Washington's War, 1779

Journal of the American Revolution Books highlight the latest research on new or lesser-known topics of the revolutionary era. The *Journal of the American Revolution* is an online resource and annual volume that provides educational, peer-reviewed articles by professional historians and experts in American Revolution studies.

A JOURNAL OF THE AMERICAN REVOLUTION BOOK

WASHINGTON'S WAR, 1779

BENJAMIN LEE HUGGINS

WESTHOLME
Yardley

To Adrina, for all her love and support

Westholme Publishing, LLC
904 Edgewood Road
Yardley, Pennsylvania 19067
Visit our Web site at www.westholmepublishing.com

ISBN: 978-1-59416-301-2
Also available as an eBook.

Printed in the United States of America.

CONTENTS

List of Maps   *vii*

Introduction   *ix*

1. A New War: Washington Becomes a True
   Commander in Chief   1
2. Provisions, Clothes, Men, Virtue, and Nation   21
3. Summer 1779: Bold Strategy but Limited War   69
4. Attack on New York: The Campaign to End
   the War   119

Conclusion   *153*

Notes   *155*

Bibliography   *175*

Acknowledgments   *179*

Index   *180*

List of Maps

1. The Greater New York City Region, 1779   XIV–XV

2. The Sullivan–Clinton Expedition,
   August–September 1779   78–79

3. The Battle of Stony Point, July 16, 1779   99

4. The Battle of Paulus Hook, August 19, 1779   109

INTRODUCTION

O N October 7, 1779, at the height of his planning for an allied attack on New York, General George Washington, commander in chief of the armies of the United States, urgently appealed to French vice admiral Charles-Hector Théodat comte d'Estaing to bring his fleet and soldiers to New York without delay:

> If your Excellency will engage to cooperate with your whole Naval and land force against the Enemy's fleet and Army at New York, till the Winter is so far advanced, that the ice will make it impracticable to remain with your fleet any longer in port, I will bring Twenty five Thousand effective Men into the Field, and will exert all the resources of the Country in a vigorous and decided co-operation.

This image of the American commander and his way of war is in stark contrast with most historians' accounts. For instance, a recent biographer has characterized 1779 as "the war's most sluggish" period and asserted that Washington, in "a limbo of inaction," had assumed a "defensive posture" and that the campaign of 1779, aside from attacks on Stony Point, New York, and Paulus Hook, New Jersey, was "uneventful." Another historian has described the commander in chief in this period as "cautious," "hesitant to engage the enemy," "uncertain of his own judgment," and plagued by "habitual indecision."

Most historians have considered the campaign of 1779 as "the forgotten war." They have skipped from the Battle of Monmouth in 1778 to the Battle of Yorktown in 1781, pausing only briefly to mention Stony Point, Paulus Hook (sometimes) in 1779, and Benedict Arnold's treason in 1780. Some have given attention to the expedition against the Iroquois in 1779. In their rush to get to Yorktown, few have paused to examine the commander in chief's plans for his army's cooperation with the French in the campaign of 1779. Apparently because Washington's plans for the campaign were never executed, historians have decided they hold nothing of interest. But a thorough reading of Washington's correspondence in the fall of 1779 uncovers a different story. Closer study reveals a different General Washington and a different type of war than that commonly portrayed by historians. Washington in the fall of 1779, far from being in a "limbo" of inactivity and indecision, planned and put into motion his boldest endeavor: a decisive, war-winning campaign to drive the British army out of New York.

A complete understanding of Washington's generalship is crucial to study of the American Revolution. The year 1779 presents an opportunity to examine many aspects of Washington's generalship, from strategic and operational planning to logistics to diplomacy.

If he had failed as a general, the Revolution most likely would have failed with him. With this book I hope to contribute to that fuller comprehension. Though the expedition against New York never took place, Washington's preparations for the allied offensive have much to tell us about his generalship. Examination of his campaign plans provides insights into his goals, his strategy, his manner of planning, his conception of potential allied operations, his ideas on employment of resources in men and material, and his vision of the capabilities of his army—in short, his way of war in the critical years between Monmouth and Yorktown.

As a micro-history, the book's central focus will be on Washington's effort to arrange a Franco-American campaign to defeat the British at New York in the fall of 1779. But it will also detail the other operations of the war in 1779, with an emphasis on Washington's generalship and how it had evolved since the early years of the war. Most historians recognize that Washington's instinct was always for offensive action, but the year 1779 has been overlooked as evidence of that trait. It should not be. Given power by Congress to plan and execute operations with the French on a continental scale, Washington carried out attacks where he could, and when it appeared that the French would bring a fleet and army to America, Washington planned his boldest campaign. The American commander proposed to attack the bastion of British power in North America—New York City—and capture its garrison. Such a blow, he hoped, would end the war in 1779. Historians have failed to give proper attention to Washington's highly detailed plans and extensive preparations for this potentially decisive campaign. Though the French defeat at Savannah, Georgia, prevented him from carrying out the offensive, Washington gained valuable experience in planning for joint operations that would help him win at Yorktown two years later.

One goal of this book is to show how, despite great limits of money, manpower, and supplies, Washington sought to wage an aggressive war in 1779 that belies the notion, propagated by some historians, of him as a Fabius, merely trying to outlast the British. It will also show that there was a great deal of fighting between the battles of Monmouth in 1778 and Yorktown in 1781. In addition to launching a campaign against the Iroquois and attacking British outposts at Stony Point and Paulus Hook, Washington planned and was ready to execute a joint Franco-American campaign to drive the British out of New York and win the war. The book will also touch on Washington's arrangements to gain intelligence in support of the offensive through the use of his Culper spy network—an intelligence network crucial to all of the general's subsequent operations.

Each chapter will cover one phase of Washington's war in 1779. Chapter one will set the stage for the operations narrated in chapters three and four. A brief overview of Washington's first campaign with the French in the summer of 1778, where his diplomacy proved crucial to preserving the military alliance, will be followed by a short

look at the origins of the Culper spy ring. It will then look at the new
war of 1779 that did not roam over multiple states as in 1776, 1777,
and 1778 but instead concentrated on the Hudson River Highlands
and New York City. Finally, another event critical for understanding
Washington's war in 1779 will be reviewed: his important meetings
with Congress in the winter that confirmed his authority as commander in chief.

Chapter two, a thematic chapter covering all of 1779, will examine Washington's views on and how he attempted to deal with the
army's lack of manpower, provisions, and clothing. It will also show
his outlook on the nation and the world situation. If the reader desires to maintain the narrative of the military actions of the war in
1779, he or she can pass over this chapter and nothing in the narrative will be lost. But the reader who takes the time to read the chapter
will gain insights into Washington's outlook and perspective on
events as well as how he dealt with the constant crises of provisions
shortages, lack of clothing, and insufficient manpower.

Chapter three looks at British and American operations in the
spring and summer of 1779—British raids in Virginia, the Hudson
Highlands, and Connecticut; and Washington's attacks on Stony
Point, New York, and Paulus Hook, New Jersey, on the Hudson
River. That summer Washington also launched an expedition against
the Iroquois in western New York. There was no period of inactivity
in 1779. Washington, despite limitations in men, money, and provisions, sought to strike his enemy where he could.

Finally, chapter four will detail Washington's design, in cooperation with a French fleet, to carry out a decisive offensive in the fall
against the British army in New York City. He sought to bring all
available resources of men and material to bear to achieve a major
victory in 1779—a victory he hoped would end the war.

For Washington's evolution as a general, 1779 was one of the
most important years of the war. In that year, he matured from a
mere army commander to a commander in chief. On September 26,
1779, Congress notified Washington that a French fleet had arrived
off the Georgia coast. Expecting that the French admiral would soon
come north for combined operations with the American commander

in chief, Congress referred "the whole system of co-operation" to Washington's direction and authorized him to "concert and execute" any plans with the French he thought proper and to call on the states for any aid in militia and supplies he might require. In short, Congress simply vested Washington with complete power to plan and execute any operations anywhere on the continent with as many men as he could put in the field. This trust in General Washington represented a vast contrast from just a year and a half before when Congress diminished his position as general by the appointment of a Board of War under his rival, Maj. Gen. Horatio Gates, with powers to set strategy, and an inspector general in Maj. Gen. Thomas Conway less than friendly to Washington. What had changed in that time? How had Washington finally become a true commander in chief? In the following pages I will attempt to answer these important questions.

Newburgh

New Windsor

West Point

Fort Montgomery   Peekskill
Fort Clinton
                    Fort Independence

British Raid 🔥   Verplanck Point
                Stony Point
            Haverstraw   White Plains

N E W   Y O R K

                                        HUDSON (NORTH) RIVER
        Orangetown
        (Tappan)

N E W   J E R S E Y

                Liberty Pole   Eastchester
                            Kingsbridge
                    Fort Knyphausen
            Fort Lee   Westchester
        New Bridge   Morrisani

    Hackinsack
                                    Flushing   Whitestone

    Newark   Paulus New
                Hook   York   Jamaica
                Bergen
                    Brooklyn
                        Bedford
Elizabethtown
                Flatbush

        Richmond   Gravesend   JAMAICA BAY
                STATEN ISLAND
    Amboy
        Billops Point

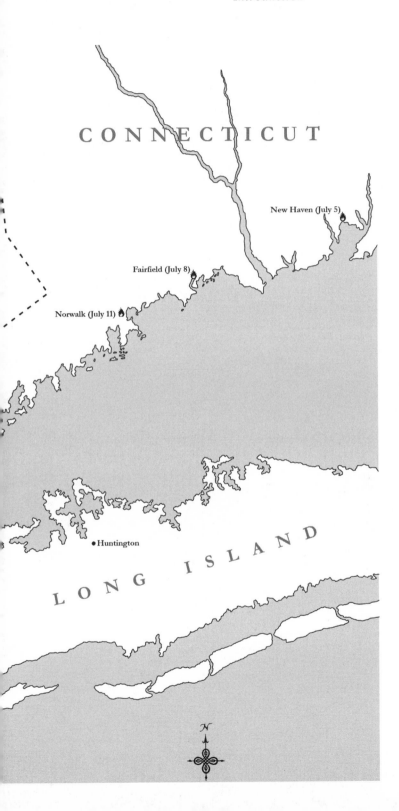

A New War: Washington Becomes a True Commander in Chief

"Congress have the most unlimited Confidence in his Wisdom
& Judgement as well As his Zeal and Integrity."
—James Duane, writing to Philip Schuyler about
George Washington, February 20, 1779

ON JUNE 28, 1778, AT MONMOUTH, NEW JERSEY, GENERAL
George Washington's Continental army engaged General Sir
Henry Clinton's British army in a daylong battle in sweltering heat.
Washington engaged Clinton's rear guard as Clinton's army sought
to withdraw from Philadelphia across New Jersey to their base in
New York City. In a very hard-fought battle, Washington, after the
repulse of the vanguard corps led by Maj. Gen. Charles Lee, took
personal charge of the army and fought a well-executed defensive
battle. Fighting in brutal heat, the Continentals proved the equal of
the British regulars. The Americans held the field at the end of the
day, but Clinton succeeded in getting his army into New York. Washington's personal leadership in the battle was crucial to American

success. Though the battle was a draw, it was portrayed in Congress and the Patriot newspapers as a grand victory. Washington's loyal officers—particularly Alexander Hamilton and John Laurens—launched a highly successful propaganda campaign to portray the battle as a great triumph. Thanks to that effort, Washington's reputation as a general was greatly enhanced. As historian Mark Lender points out, "the official version of the Monmouth campaign erased public questions about his leadership." As Lender observes: "Washington emerged from the Monmouth campaign with his critics cowed into silence, his potential rivals in the officer corps routed . . . and his military acumen praised in terms fit for Alexander."[1]

Although Monmouth solidified Washington's position as general, he had not yet become a true commander in chief. Though holding that title, he was not yet in command of all regional departments of the army and Congress still held control of strategy. It would take the arrival of French forces to make him a true commander in chief. Washington would then by necessity become the coordinator of allied military and naval operations.

In February 1778, France joined the war by signing an alliance with the United States. The alliance, specifically the arrival of French forces to cooperate with the Continental army, meant that Washington had to expand his skills as a general beyond just the command of a single army. He would have to engage in cooperation with allied forces sent to America and conduct relations with the commanders of those forces. He proved equal to the task.

Vice Admiral d'Estaing's fleet of twelve ships of the line and five frigates departed Toulon, France, on April 13, 1778.[2] A body of troops embarked on the fleet. Congress learned on July 10 of the presence of the French fleet off the coast, bound for Sandy Hook, New Jersey, and the entrance to the Bay of New York. They immediately notified Washington and directed him to send a letter to the French admiral "where it may reach him, & you will also concert measures for improving the force under Your Excellency's immediate Command & that under the direction of Maj. Gen. Gates, in the present critical conjuncture."[3] Washington, camped with the main army at Paramus, New Jersey, received the letter three days later and immediately dispatched his aide-de-camp Lt. Col. John Laurens (who spoke French) with a letter from the general to Vice Admiral d'Estaing. Washington put his army in motion toward the Hudson River where, he informed Congress, "I shall pursue such measures as may appear best calculated for improving the present conjuncture."[4]

On July 11, the day following the arrival of the intelligence of d'Estaing's presence on the coast, Congress granted large powers to Washington to plan and conduct combined operations with the French and to call for militia in such numbers as "he shall think requisite" from New Hampshire, Massachusetts, Rhode Island, Connecticut, New York, and New Jersey "for carrying on his operations in concert with Count d'Estaing." Congress desired Washington to cooperate with d'Estaing "in the Execution of such offensive operations against the Enemy as shall appear to be necessary."[5] Congress's "appear to be necessary" language gave wide latitude to Washington to plan and execute combined operations.[6]

Realizing the great importance to his operations of having a French fleet to cooperate with him, Washington quickly dispatched a letter to the French admiral proposing the formulation of a plan for joint action. He was ready to undertake cooperation immediately. "I take the earliest opportunity to advise you, that I have been informed of your arrival on this coast, with a fleet of Ships under your command, belonging to his most Christian Majesty, our Great Ally," he wrote. "I congratulate you, Sir, most sincerely upon this event and beg leave to assure you of my warmest wishes for your success." Washington relayed his best intelligence on the number of British ships of war in the port of New York and advised the French admiral that he had "now arrived with the main body of the Army, immediately under my command, within twenty miles of the North or Hudson's river, which I mean to pass as soon as possible about fifty miles above New York. I shall then move down before the Enemy's lines, with a view of giving them every jealousy in my power. And I further think it proper to assure you, that I shall upon every occasion feel the strongest inclination to facilitate such enterprizes as you may form and are pleased to communicate to me." Washington also saw an important way to utilize the newly arrived fleet: "I have just received advice, that the Enemy are in daily expectation of a provision fleet from Cork, and that they are under great apprehensions, lest it should fall into your hands."[7] The destruction of the supply fleet from Cork, Ireland, would result in extreme hardship in New York City because the garrison could not meet all its needs from locally obtained provision and forage.

The French admiral had already written to Washington from his flagship "At sea." The letter was carried ashore by the admiral's aide-de-camp Major André-Michel-Victor, marquis de Chouin. D'Estaing couched his announcement in diplomatic terms:

> I have the honor of imparting to Your Excelly the arrival of the King's fleet; charged by his Majesty with the glorious task of giving his allies the United States of America the most striking proofs of his affection. Nothing will be wanting to my happiness if I can succeed in it; it is augmented by the consideration of concerting my operations with a General such as Your Excellency. The talents and great actions of General Washington have insured him in the eyes of all Europe, the title, truly sublime deliverer of America. Accept Sir, the homage that every man—that every military man owes you; and be not displeased, that I solicit, even in the first moment of intercourse, with military and maritime frankness, a friendship so flattering as yours. I will try to render myself worthy of it by my respectful devotion for your country; it is prescribed to me by orders, and my heart inspires it.[8]

D'Estaing followed this letter with a second one encouraging Washington to propose a plan for military cooperation. "The first moments are so pretious, above all upon Sea, that it may be of the greatest importance for me to be informed four and twenty hours sooner or later of the projects of Your Excellency," he advised. "I have orders to second them; I dare assure you, that I will do it to the utmost of my power. To act in concert with a great man is the first of blessings—tis one of those which flatter me the most in the commission with which I am honored."[9] Such a proposal for immediate joint action could only please the American general.

On the night of July 14, Washington received d'Estaing's letters. Almost immediately, he began formulating strategy and plans. Taking several days to make some arrangements for the fleet before answering the admiral's letter and sending his aide Lt. Col. John Laurens to meet him, Washington sent a very diplomatic response to the Frenchman:

> The arrival of a fleet, belonging to his most Christian majesty on our coast, is an event that makes me truly happy; and permit me to observe, that the pleasure I feel on the occasion is greatly increased, by the command being placed in a Gentleman of such distinguished talents, experience and reputation as the Count D'Estaing. I am fully persuaded that every possible exertion will be made by you to accomplish the important purposes of your destination, and you may have the firmest reliance, that my most strenuous efforts shall accompany you in any measure, which may be found eligible.
>
> I esteem myself highly honored by the desire you express, with a frankness which must always be pleasing, of possessing a place in my friendship; At the same time allow me to assure you, that I shall consider myself peculiarly happy, if I can but improve the prepossessions you are pleased to entertain in my favour, into a cordial and lasting amity.

He hoped d'Estaing would entrust Laurens with "your situation and views, so far as might be proper for my direction in any measures of concert or cooperation, which may be thought advancive of the common cause." Chouin had given him "a very full and satisfactory explanation" of d'Estaing's ideas for joint action. In return, the American commander had "freely communicated to him my ideas of every matter interesting to our mutual operations." Since receiving d'Estaing's letters, Washington had been collecting information "essential to the formation of our plans." He dispatched his aide-de-camp Lt. Col. Alexander Hamilton in whom, he advised the admiral, he placed "entire confidence." Hamilton would, he assured d'Estaing, "be able to make you perfectly acquainted with my sentiments, and to satisfy any inquiries you may think proper to propose; and I would wish you to consider the information he delivers as coming from my self." Washington sent pilots and knowledgeable ship captains familiar with the coast and harbors to aid the French captains with navigation.[10]

Washington realized the importance of successful allied cooperation. "Interest and policy strongly press us to cooperate with, and to give every countenance to our Friends upon this occasion; and this is the wish of Congress," he declared to General Gates, at this period commanding the Continental army brigades already in New York. He directed Gates to make the enemy in New York aware of the motions of the army; he was to circulate a report "in a proper manner" that they were on the point of concentrating the army for an attack against New York. "This will excite the Enemy's fears, and . . . may greatly facilitate the Admiral's designs and produce the most beneficial consequences. We should attempt to rouse their jealousy in every quarter, and in every shape."[11] Washington asserted to Connecticut governor Jonathan Trumbull, "Every thing we can do to aid and cooperate with this Fleet is of the greatest importance." He again raised the issue of an attack on the Cork fleet, suggesting that "it might answer the most valuable consequences" if the New England states would collect all the frigates and armed vessels they could gather and strike the supply fleet if it entered Long Island Sound. "If the whole, or any considerable part of the Cork-Fleet could be taken or destroyed, it would be a fatal blow to the British Army, which, it is supposed, at this time, has but a very small stock of Provisions on hand."[12]

In his next letter, as his ships waited outside the bar at Sandy Hook, New Jersey, while his pilots sounded the depth to determine if his ships could enter, d'Estaing insisted to Washington that "so great a naval succour" as his fleet should produce "a general effort by land." If Washington could not provide forces for such a cooperation, the admiral advised the American general that "necessity" would then force him "to seek elsewhere an opportunity of injuring our common enemy." But he expressed "the greatest pleasure that Congress had vested Washington with "the most ample powers" to plan and conduct joint military operations.[13]

If d'Estaing feared that Washington hesitated to use the Continental army for cooperation with the French fleet in joint operations, his fears were groundless. The American general wanted to "be ready at all points, and for all events" for cooperative operations with the French.[14] He was already thinking of major operations involving the fleet and the Continental army. He informed Maj. Gen. John Sullivan, commanding in Rhode Island: "No particular plan is yet adopted, but two seem to present themselves; either an attack upon New York, or Rhode Island." He considered his army "very well disposed" for an operation against New York, if it was found "practicable." Anticipating that the French admiral might opt for the Rhode Island operation and using the authority granted him by Congress, Washington directed Sullivan to apply to the executives of Rhode Island, Massachusetts, and Connecticut to form a body of five thousand militiamen to reinforce the troops already in Rhode Island.[15]

When d'Estaing found that he could not get his ships over the bar of New York Bay, he and Washington quickly shifted the campaign to a joint attack on the British force at Newport, Rhode Island. D'Estaing departed Sandy Hook and sailed for Rhode Island and Narragansett Bay for the combined operation. The admiral, Lieutenant Colonel Hamilton informed Washington, "wishes not a moment may be lost. . . . He begs every thing may be forwarded as much as possible; and as many troops collected as may be. He would be glad a detachment could march from your army."[16]

When d'Estaing decided for the Rhode Island operation, Washington put absolute priority on the Rhode Island "Enterprize." He ordered two Continental brigades, totaling about two thousand men, to Providence under the command of Maj. Gen. Marie-Joseph-Paul-Yves-Roch-Gilbert du Motier, marquis de Lafayette.[17] He informed d'Estaing that immediately on learning of the shift to Rhode Island he had ordered this reinforcement sent to Sullivan "that he might be in a situation for a vigorous co-operation." He expressed his pleasure in finding that they agreed "so exactly in the importance of this expedition."[18] Advising Lafayette of his intention to send Maj. Gen. Nathanael Greene to Rhode Island, Washington emphasized the importance of the allied attack on Newport: "The honor and interest of the common cause are so deeply concerned in the success of this enterprise, that it appears to me of the greatest importance to omit no step which may conduce to it." Greene, a native of Rhode Island, would, he explained, be "particularly useful" to the expedition and would assist the other generals in formulating and executing a plan of operations. He directed that the Continentals and militia should be formed together and divided into two divisions with Lafayette to command one and Greene the other. General Sullivan, senior to both officers, would command the whole.[19] Washington remained in New York with the bulk of the army to watch the British main force in New York City and its environs.[20] With Sullivan, Greene, and Lafayette commanding the American forces in Rhode Island, diplomacy soon became Washington's primary task in the campaign.

For a top-level military leader in a coalition, maintaining good relations with his allies is of the first importance. With the signing of the military alliance with France in 1778, Washington had to add this role to his generalship. As soon as d'Estaing arrived with his naval squadron to cooperate with his army, the American commander had to become a diplomat. Their exchange of letters on d'Estaing's arrival already showed that Washington was aware of this newly necessary part of his generalship.

During the Rhode Island campaign of 1778, Washington's diplomacy saved the fledgling Franco-American alliance. From the beginning of the campaign, Washington recognized the importance of accord between the allied forces. "Harmony & the best understanding between us, should be a Capital & first Object," he reminded General Sullivan.[21]

Sullivan and d'Estaing planned to land their respective forces on Rhode (Aquidneck) Island and in a joint offensive drive the British from Newport. But after a promising start to the campaign, d'Estaing, with several ships damaged in a storm and facing the threat of a superior British fleet, chose to withdraw his squadron from Rhode Island waters to Boston. There he could safely repair and refit his ships. Reacting angrily to the French strategic decision, Sullivan's senior officers issued a "Protest" that declared "the Honor of the French

Nation . . . injured by their Fleet abandoning their Allies." (Lafayette refused to sign the protest and Greene apparently had no part in it.)[22] Sullivan followed this protest by writing a letter to the officers in which he accused d'Estaing of "having abandoned us." The next day he issued a general order in which he accused the French of failing the "great dependance" the Americans had placed on their assistance. As might be expected, the allied commanders-in-chief did not react well to these rash pronouncements. Washington thought Sullivan's order had been "very impolitic."[23] Lafayette, in two long letters, explained the French point of view. The French admiral, he reported, was "much displeas'd" by the protest. He assured Washington that d'Estaing was "distress'd" that he had been prevented from striking a blow against the British. Lafayette lamented "the ungenerous sentiments I have been forc'd to see in Many American breasts." He complained of "the most horrid ungratefulness." Personally, the situation "afflicted" Lafayette "as an american, and as a frenchman together."[24]

In this potentially damaging situation, Washington's overarching concern, even over the success or failure of the Newport expedition, became protection of the French alliance. To Greene, he wrote that unless "the most prudent measures" were "taken to suppress the feuds and jealousies that have already arisen" he feared that d'Estaing's departure for Boston could "sow the seeds of dissention and distrust between us and our new allies."[25] He could not allow public censure of the French that would hazard the partnership, and he so instructed Sullivan and Maj. Gen. William Heath at Boston. According to Washington, "at so critical a moment" the situation had to be "prudently managed" to avoid "injurious consequences" to the alliance. "Sound policy" required that they "give the most favorable construction, of what has happened, to the public" and attribute the French withdrawal to "necessity."[26] Following a policy determined by Congress, Washington even asked Greene to "take every measure" to keep the protest from being made public.[27]

The American commander then took a personal hand in resolving the crisis. He called on his generals to protect the military partnership with France. For the sake of the all-important alliance, Washington urged Heath to become a diplomat and use his "utmost influence to palliate and soften matters." He also appealed to Greene: "I depend much upon your temper and influence to conciliate that animosity which I plainly perceive . . . subsists between the American Officers and the French in our service." He asked him to exert himself "to heal all private animosities between our principal Officers and the French, and to prevent all illiberal expressions and reflections that may fall from the Army at large."[28] To Sullivan, Washington revealed his deep concern for the preservation of the coalition. The disagreement had given him what he termed a "very singular uneasiness." "The Continent at large is concerned in our cordiality," he wrote, "and it should be kept up by all possible means that are consistent with our honor and policy. First impressions, you know, are generally longest remembered, and will serve to fix in a great degree our national character among the French. Permit me to recommend in the most particular manner, the cultivation of harmony and good agreement."

With this carefully crafted letter, Washington showed Sullivan that maintenance of the alliance far outweighed concerns over the forced retreat from Rhode Island and any strategic moves of the French squadron.

The general considered placating Lafayette, the senior Frenchman in American service, particularly important. To General Greene he explained: "if he can be pacified, the other French Gentlemen will of course be satisfied as they look up to him as their Head." Leaving nothing to chance, Washington wrote to Lafayette himself. The letter is at once instructive and diplomatic:

But in one word, let me say, I feel every thing that hurts the sensibility of a Gentleman; and, consequently, upon the present occasion, feel for you & for our good & great Allys the French—I feel myself hurt also at every illiberal, and unthinking reflection which may have been cast upon Count D'Estaing, or the conduct of the Fleet under his command. and lastly, I feel for my Country. Let me entreat you therefore my dear Marquis to take no exception at unmeaning expressions, uttered perhaps without Consideration, & in the first transport of disappointed hope—Every

body Sir, who reasons, will acknowledge the advantages which we
have derived from the French Fleet, & the Zeal of the Commander
of it, but in a free, & republican Government, you cannot restrain
the voice of the multitude—every Man will speak as he thinks, or
more properly without thinking. . . . The censures which have
been levelled at the Officers of the French Fleet, would, more than
probable, have fallen in a much higher degree upon a Fleet of our
own (if we had had one) in the same situation. . . . Let me beseech
you therefore my good Sir to afford a healing hand to the wound
that, unintentially, has been made. America esteems your Virtues
& yr Services—and admires the principles upon which you act.
Your Countrymen, in our Army, look up to you as their Patron.
The Count and his Officers consider you as a man high in Rank,
& high in estimation, here and in France; and I, your friend, have
no doubt but that you will use your utmost endeavours to restore
harmony that the honour, glory, and mutual Interest of the two
Nation's may be promoted and cemented in the firmest manner.[29]

Letting his generals conduct the local diplomacy with the French,
Washington took a statesmanlike approach to d'Estaing's withdrawal. He ignored the controversy and focused on his chief concern:
keeping the French fleet in American waters. "The importance of the
fleet under your command to the common cause and the interest I
take in your personal concerns," he wrote to the admiral, "would
not permit me, but to be deeply affected with the information of the
disappointment and injuries you sustained in the late unfortunate
storm. I flatter myself, and I most ardently hope, my countrymen will
exert themselves to give you every aid in their power, that you may
as soon as possible recover from the damage you have suffered and
be in a condition to renew your efforts against the common enemy."
D'Estaing's final words on the incident reveal the effectiveness of the
general's diplomatic policy. The French commander told Washington
that he remained "devoted to the common cause, and the union of
the two nations," and he graciously credited the general's letters with
smoothing over the crisis, assuring the American commander that
Sullivan's words were "intirely forgotten."[30] Although Washington's

diplomacy managed to heal the dispute before it became a threat to the alliance, Sullivan had been forced to conduct a fighting retreat from Aquidneck Island, a successful operation for which he rightly received praise, even from Lafayette.[31]

The arrival of a French naval force brought with it the need for better intelligence of British naval movements. Washington, dissatisfied with his current sources of intelligence, had to set up a new spy network. Recognizing provision of accurate intelligence for the French as a critical aspect of the new military alliance, he sought trustworthy spies to gather quality information. Washington required reliable intelligence—particularly naval intelligence—for the two commanders to counter British operations. In September 1778, with the French squadron refitting and resupplying at Boston, d'Estaing anticipated a British move against his fleet. He pressed the American commander for intelligence on British intentions. "In order to counteract the enemy's projects, it is essential to penetrate them without loss of time," d'Estaing advised Washington, "it is impossible to employ money more usefully than on this object—and I would readily engage for the Kings Share of the expence of Spies—in order to act [it] is essential to have intelligence."[32] Three days later, the French admiral gave Washington a list of the kind of information he required—the kind and number of British ships in New York, the condition of the ships, the state of the British army in the New York City area, and "the insight which may be gained of their designs." On this intelligence "will depend our offensive or defensive plans." "Good Spies," he advised, "must be the basis of all."[33]

Washington realized that British naval superiority would force the allies to suspend their plans for offensive cooperation. At the same time, he recognized the importance of defending the French from British attack by land or sea. "It is of infinite importance that we should take all the means that our circumstances will allow for the defence of a Squadron, which is so pretious to the common cause of France and America." He assured the French commander that he recognized the "necessity of having intelligent spies" to aid in the formulation of allied plans. "Every measure that circumstances would admit has been taken to answer this valuable end, and has in general been as good as could be expected from the situation of the enemy."[34]

Despite these assurances, Washington remained dissatisfied with his existing espionage system. He already had spies sending in intelligence on British naval and army movements, but their reports proved inadequate for the admiral's requirements. His need for *accurate and reliable* intelligence on enemy naval operations to pass to d'Estaing led the American general to establish the famous Culper spy ring. After receiving d'Estaing's letters, Washington directed Brigadier General Charles Scott, commander of the light infantry corps (stationed near the British lines), and who already managed spies in New York, "to get an intelligent person into the City, & others of *his own choice* to be Messengers between you and him, for conveying such information as he shall be able to obtain & give. It is of great consequence to the French Admiral to be early, & regularly advised of the movements of the British Ships of War, at New York; and he depends upon me to give this advice." "Vague & idle stories" were unacceptable. False intelligence might prove worse than none. The new spy "should therefore examine well into, & compare matters before he transmits acc[oun]ts; always distinguishing facts of his own knowledge from reports. If Mr C——- [Culper; alias of the Culper spy Abraham Woodhull] could be engaged in a Work of this sort, his discernment, & mean of information, would enable him to give important advices."[35]

Washington, Scott, and Maj. Benjamin Tallmadge, who became the direct manager of the Culper spies, had their new network functioning in a month. The first known intelligence from the Culper ring gave the detailed, quality intelligence needed for d'Estaing: a fleet supposedly sailing to the West Indies with a newly raised corps; the date of embarkation of a provincial brigade; Maj. Gen. William Tryon's movements; and heavy cannon loaded onboard the ships.[36] But with little prospect for operations with Washington until the summer, d'Estaing changed the focus of his operations. He had learned that a British fleet carrying a large number of troops was bound for the West Indies with obvious designs on valuable French islands in that region. In early November, with his ships repaired, re-fitted, and resupplied, d'Estaing sailed for the West Indies.[37]

By the end of November, even though d'Estaing had departed for the Caribbean, Washington was sure the Culper network fit his needs, remarking to Major Tallmadge that a report from Culper had "the appearance of a distinct and good one, and makes me desirous of a continuance of his correspondence."[38] With a genesis in the needs of Vice Adm. d'Estaing, the Culper spy ring continued to serve Washington well throughout the remainder of the war.

The Rhode Island campaign, though militarily unfruitful, proved critical to building Washington as commander in chief. He had proven his ability to conduct joint operations and maintain harmonious relations with his French counterpart—two critical facets of being commander in chief. In the summer and fall of 1778 Washington solidified his position as general and had begun to establish himself as commander in chief in a military alliance. The coming year would see that evolution completed. With the coming of the new year, the war entered a new phase.

With the departure of d'Estaing for the West Indies, the war's focus became the Hudson River. Even as Washington planned the disposition of his army in the late summer of 1778 he took into account the vital importance of the Hudson. As he explained the situation to the French admiral: "Almost all our supplies of flour, and no inconsiderable part of our meat, are drawn from the States westward of Hudsons River—this renders a secure communication across that River indispensibly necessary not only to the support of the Army, but the valuable Squadron of His most Christian Majesty, if it should be blocked up by a superior fleet—the enemy being masters of that navigation would interrupt this essential intercourse between the States." He viewed securing the Hudson River as one of "two great ends" to take account of in his dispositions (the other, at that time, being the defense of d'Estaing's fleet).[39]

In 1779 the Hudson River region became the central theater of the war. The British controlled New York City and its environs, including Staten Island, Long Island, and the outpost of Paulus Hook directly opposite New York City (in addition to Newport, Rhode Island). With their navy controlling New York Bay, the lower Hudson River, and the East River, the British could easily shift troops among these various outposts and quickly assemble regiments for expeditions. The Continental army held the Hudson Highlands, with its vital post of West Point, and the forts guarding the important river crossing at King's Ferry.

By the beginning of 1779, both sides had begun to perceive New York and the Hudson River Highlands as the key to the war. The British peace commissioners, the Earl of Carlisle and William Eden, just back in England from their failed effort in Philadelphia in 1778, advised, according to historian Piers Mackesy, "the New York area as the starting point of political re-absorption; and their suggested occupation of the [Hudson] Highlands would have the further military advantage of cutting New England off from supplies and succour." British general James Robertson also viewed the Highlands as "the vital country." Robertson believed occupation of the Highlands could starve the Continental army (it drew much beef supplies from New England), open communications with Indians on the frontier, and allow Loyalists in the area to organize a militia.[40] Washington considered West Point the most important post in America.[41] The fortress guarded the link across the Hudson between New York and New England and denied the British access to the upper Hudson. Only two Hudson River crossings remained in American hands—West Point and King's Ferry. Since the main British army was stationed in the New York City area, West Point was the last line of defense for this vital link. If West Point and King's Ferry were lost, New England would be isolated and its supplies of provisions and men to the Continental army lost. Washington could not allow that to happen. While the loss of King's Ferry would mean longer marches and transportation routes, the loss of West Point could be fatal to the cause. West Point, he knew, must be defended at all costs. At the beginning of the winter of 1779, Washington deployed his army in an arc from northern New Jersey to the east side of the Hudson to defend the Highlands.

New York City was the center of British army operations on the continent. The largest part of their army in the Americas was posted in the New York City area. Many of the military reinforcements for the West Indies and Canada embarked from New York. Any major expedition by the British commander in chief would be launched from that post. The garrison of New York sheltered a large colony of Loyalist refugees from the nearby states. A line of defensive works guarded the approaches to the city on the north and the British maintained forts in the north end of Manhattan Island, at King's Bridge (guarding the crossing into mainland New York) in Westchester County, and at Brooklyn on Long Island to protect the city. Even though the main naval base in the Americas was Halifax, Nova Scotia, the navy maintained a squadron of sixty-four-gun ships and frigates at New York.

Clinton's position at New York and Long Island was strong, but it suffered from two grave potential weaknesses, both involving control of the oceans: his forces at New York were totally dependent on the regular arrival of the supply fleets from Great Britain and the safety of his outlying garrisons, and even the garrison of New York depended on maintaining naval superiority. These were weaknesses that Washington had recognized.

These two bastions of British and American power—West Point and New York—became the focus of the two commanders in chief: defending the one and taking the other. In 1779, operations began to focus on these two bastions because their capture would be decisive. With a decisive victory in the field looking elusive after three campaigns, both sides looked to the capture of these key bases as another way to end the war.

Washington began 1779 in discussions with a committee of the Continental Congress. With his army encamped in winter quarters, the general was able to travel to Philadelphia for the conference. He had asked for the meeting to resolve strategy in regard to an expedition to Canada, which he opposed. The series of meetings lasted for over one month—from December 24, 1778, to February 1, 1779. The general quickly persuaded Congress to set aside the Canada invasion plan.[42] He and the committee then proceeded to examine all aspects of army administration and strategy. In January, he submitted two papers on "the general operations of the next Campaign."[43]

In his first paper, Washington covered recruiting, strategy, ordnance, clothing, and the hospital department. "The first and great object is to recruit the Army," he wrote. No bounty should be spared to expand the enlistments of all the men then in the army to the duration of the war. If successful, such action would end the need to recruit new troops every year and would increase the professionalism of the army. He proposed two plans of operations for 1779: one against New York City and Rhode Island, and the other against Niagara, the center of British power in the west. If Congress's finances could support a campaign against New York and Rhode Island, he argued, "we ought to direct almost our whole force and exertions to that point." A diversionary expedition against Detroit would protect the frontiers. If Congress could not finance the complimentary expedition against Niagara, it should be dropped and all efforts concentrated on New York and Rhode Island. "To determine therefore what we can undertake—the state of the army the prospect of recruiting it—paying, cloathing and feeding it—the providing the necessary apparatus for offensive operations—all these matters ought to be well and maturely considered. On them every thing must depend." But, he asked the committee, would not the depreciation of the Continental currency, the lack of bread, the scarcity of forage, and the exhausted state of the resources in the middle states make it advisable to remain on the defensive with the main force of the army and conduct only an expedition in the west against the Indians? "It is in vain to attempt things which are more the objects of desire than attainment. Every undertaking must be, at least ought to be, regulated by the state of our finances, the prospect of our supplies and the probability of success." He then gave the committee a preliminary analysis of the administrative challenges facing the army and his view of the best arrangements for the artillery, ordnance, and engineers.[44] The committee was impressed with this first memorandum. "We therefore request that you will be pleased to point out what ought to be done with respect to the Arrangement of the Army—the Department of Artillery & Ordinance—the Cloathing Departmt the Inspectorship & the Branch of Engineers," committeeman James Duane wrote to him. "Indeed we think it woud be adviseable to vest the Commander in Chief with power to make these & every other Arrangement for the good Government of the Army by forming a compleat System to be adopted by Congress as their Act."[45]

In a letter to a committee member written shortly before he submitted his second paper on campaign strategy for 1779, Washington, undoubtedly frustrated by his lack of control over all the affairs and departments of the army, called for "a controuling power" over all departments of the army "to preserve harmony and correspondence in the system of the Army." The orders of Congress and the Board of War "to any department or Officer," he asserted, should go through the commander in chief. Otherwise "collision of orders and confusion in affairs will be the inevitable consequence."[46] The committee, and Congress, would soon act on this recommendation.

In his second, and more extensive, paper on strategy for the coming campaign Washington put forward three alternative plans, each with their governing considerations, advantages, and drawbacks. He discussed the practicability of each. In his first plan, he proposed a campaign by the main army against New York and Newport, Rhode Island. This plan he viewed as "the most desirable," he told the committee, "because if it could succeed, it would be decisive." But it had drawbacks. Washington pointed out that the central position of the British posts in New York, the strength of their forts, and their ability to move troops by water to reinforce any of their posts were "obstacles not easily to be overcome." He estimated it would require twenty-six thousand effective troops—a larger number than they had ever put into the field—and he warned of the difficulty and expense of supplying so large an army.

Washington proposed as his second plan an expedition against Fort Niagara with an expeditionary force of seven to eight thousand troops to "give effectual security to our Frontier and open a door into Canada." A defensive force of thirteen thousand men would be left in lower New York and the Hudson Highlands. Though this plan required fewer troops, the object was less and it risked almost as much as the first plan and might exhaust the country's resources in "distant and indecisive Expeditions."

As a third option Washington proposed to keep the main army "intirely on the defensive" and send an expedition against the hostile nations of the Iroquois confederation "to divert their ravages from us." He remarked that because the prospects for any "capital offensive" seemed "so slender," they appeared driven to the "necessity" of adopting this third plan. But this plan had advantages: it would offer them the opportunity of "retrenching our expenses" and adopting a system of economy. Congress might then be able to act to restore the public credit and the value of the currency. The general feared the impact on the campaign of the rapidly depreciating currency, "the great impediment to all vigorous measures." The army could be recruited and given "a firm and permanent texture." The plan would also offer "some repose to the Country" and thus help relieve the scarcity of food supplies. Five days after Washington submitted this paper the committee had made its decision. Accepting his judgment of the "absolute necessity of contracting our system," the committee adopted the third plan. The army would remain on the defensive in 1779 except for an expedition against the Iroquois.[47]

The committee of conference did more than just discuss strategy with Washington. Their conference extended to all the areas covered in his first memorandum. Demonstrating his mastery over army administration, the general soon submitted highly detailed papers covering almost every aspect of army administration.[48] The committee accepted almost all of Washington's recommendations.

Few historians have taken note of these meetings with the committee of Congress in the winter of 1779, but the conference was a crucial turning point in Washington's evolution as a commander. It became the foundation for his war in 1779. The meetings firmly established him as commander in chief of all the Continental army. As the coming months would show, Congress would now place all operational and strategic planning under his direction. On January 23, even before the conference concluded, Congress gave Washington complete control over military operations in every department and

placed all army affairs under his direction. Congress resolved "That
the Commander in Chief be directed to superintend and direct the
military operations in all the departments in these states, subject to
the regulations and orders of Congress." They specifically placed the
operations from Fort Pitt and the Northern Department under his
direction.[49] As the New York delegates, one a member of the committee, wrote to the governor of their state: "The operations which
will be most effectual are submitted to his Judgement, and every Department is placed under his immediate Superintendence."[50] James
Duane, a member of the committee, put it simply: "Congress have
the most unlimited Confidence in his Wisdom & Judgement as well
As his Zeal and Integrity."[51] Vested with this new authority and with
such strong backing from Congress, Washington could be confident
in carrying out plans for operations across the continent in 1779.

Two

Provisions, Clothes
Men, Virtue, and Nation

"I am alarmed and wish to see my Countrymen roused."
—Washington to Benjamin Harrison, December 18, 1778

I N 1779 A LARGE PART OF WASHINGTON'S WAR CONSISTED OF HIS
efforts to supply the army, provide transportation to move supplies, cloth the army, and maintain the army's manpower. Without
these his army could not fight and his indefatigable effort to supply
these things for his army was impressive. His perseverance in this
area was a key facet of his generalship.

Washington possessed a keen grasp of the situation of the United
States. The Continental currency constantly fell in value in 1779 and
this affected the purchase of provisions and transportation to move
them. The poor financial situation of Congress limited Washington's
operations in the first part of the year and forced him to resort to
impressment of transportation and forage to move his army. Washington also detected an apparent decline in patriotic zeal, which he
held responsible for the lack of effort by some states in providing
manpower for the army and keeping it supplied with provisions.

Washington also possessed a firm grasp of the world situation and how it would affect the campaign in North America.

Rarely did the American commander in 1779 complain of this lack of "virtue" in his public letters. He reserved his comments on the national situation for his private letters to friends and relatives. Washington's private letters give insights into his views not often presented in accounts of his war. Some of his most powerful letters—in which he expressed his views on a multitude of difficulties he faced and the country's situation—are these candid, private epistles. They provide such a unique look into Washington's view of his war that they deserve extensive quotation. In short, to understand Washington's war in 1779 one must understand his views on these issues and how he attempted to overcome these difficulties that constantly plagued him as general of the army.

Providing the army with bread and other food occupied Washington's correspondence from the beginning of the year to the end. Whether the army was stationary in camp or moving, the soldiers had to eat. Shortages were a problem in all the army's regional departments. Early in the year, Washington addressed the situation in the Western Department, at this time commanded by Brig. Gen. Lachlan McIntosh, with Congress:

> In consequence of the authority vested in me by Congress of "directing and superintending the military operations in these States," I was led to make inquiry into the State of the Magazines to the Westward. From a late letter of Genl McIntosh's to myself, and several to the Board of War, I find that he has been so much distressed for provision, that he has been obliged suddenly to disband all the Militia that were in service, and seems to be very apprehensive that he shall with difficulty subsist the two Continental Regiments and a few Independent Companies, thro' the Winter. . . . I have thought it my duty to represent this to Congress as early as possible that proper enquiries may be made of those who have hitherto had the charge of procuring supplies, whether they have made the necessary arrangements for establish-

ing Magazines at Fort Pitt in the Spring . . . I fear, notwithstanding our utmost exertions, it will be late before sufficient Magazines can be formed, especially of Flour, the Crops beyond the Alleghany having been generally lost last summer by the evacuation of the Country. The transportation of that Article therefore must be very distant. I hope Congress will view this matter in the same important light that I do, and that whatever their determination may be, it be as speedy as the Case will admit.[1]

Provision shortages also plagued the Highlands Department in New York. Writing from his headquarters at the army's encampment at Middlebrook, New Jersey, Washington wrote to the commander of the department: "The distresses of the posts under your command for the articles of flour and forage are truly embarassing—They are the more deplorable, as similar ones are felt in every other part— This camp has been, not long since, reduced to an alarming extremity for the want of forage—The truth is, there is a real scarcity of the two articles—The country is in a great degree exhausted, and our money is of so little value, that it affords hardly any temptation to the farmers to furnish what they have."[2]

The problems continued into the summer. In late August 1779, as he anticipated major operations to defend West Point, Washington addressed a circular letter to the state executives on shortages of flour. "I take the liberty and indeed I am compelled by necessity to transmit to your Excellency the copy of a letter, I received yesterday from Col. Wadsworth the Commissary General, which places our supplies of flour in a very serious and alarming point of view," he wrote.

"The subject is so very important and interesting—that I am perfectly convinced it will engage your Excellency's immediate attention—and that nothing in your power will be omitted that can contribute to our instant relief and to promote our future supplies of this essential article. I will not detail the consequences of a failure of flour at this time—they will but too sensibly strike your Excellency; but I think they may be fatal. Besides the common demands of the army it is highly probable we shall be obliged in the course of a few days to call in aid from the militia, which will increase our expenditures. . . . It is likely the deficiency may arise in a great measure from the exhausted state of the old crop and the new's not being yet threshed or carried to the mills. . . . I am satisfied you will adopt & practice every expedient that shall seem to promise relief."[3]

In December, after active campaigning had ended for 1779, Washington, with his army just having entered winter quarters, still faced extreme difficulties supplying his troops. This situation prompted a series of letters to Congress. Forwarding a letter from the commissary general of forage on shortages of that crucial item, the general declared, "I do not know what will or can be done, but I confess I am greatly alarmed at the prospect of our supplies of provision which so much depend on those of forage."[4]

Four days later Washington wrote again to Congress, "I have the honor to lay before your Excellency the inclosed papers relative to the state of our supplies of meat." He forwarded to Congress letters to him from Royal Flint, deputy commissary general of purchases, and a letter from Henry Champion to Jeremiah Wadsworth, commissary general of purchases. Champion advised Wadsworth: "You are very sensible that the want of Money for three or four Months past has been a great hindrance to Peoples purchasing and preparing to winter feed . . . [I] think it my duty thus early to acquaint You that its my sincere belief that I shall not be able to supply the Army more than two Weeks after this with fresh Meat, and even that will be very difficult unless a large supply of Cash is immediately sent or is now on the road. I mean I fear I shall not be able to start droves from here sufficient but two weeks after this . . . which will nearly be consumed in Camp by the last of this or beginning of next Month." Flint, in case the army was "reduced to a scarcity, or want of meat" and so "such an event may not come altogether unexpected," informed Washington "that the subsistence of the army is hastening to a very desperate crisis. If the difficulty [Champion] has long felt from a want of money is not soon removed . . . there is no reason to depend on a full continuance of his supplies."[5]

Two weeks later Flint sent a report to Washington's headquarters that there might soon be a sudden failure of the supplies of meat. Champion had sent him accounts "which are more unfavorable than

I could have expected," Flint relayed. But he was "not utterly without hope even though the exigence is critical and the prospects far from flattering. The resources of [Connecticut] are by no means exhausted. It is capable I presume of affording fat cattle sufficient for our subsistance several weeks. The principal point then is how are we to draw out the supplies? It would be practicable if we had *money* & I hope not impracticable though we have *none*."[6]

By December 15 the situation had become so dire that Washington once again wrote to Congress. He informed the delegates "of the deplorable distress of the great departments of the army." "I beg leave to add that from a particular consultation of the Commissaries," he continued. "I find our prospects are infinitely worse than they have been at any period of the War, and that unless some expedient can be instantly adopted a dissolution of the army for want of subsistence is unavoidable—A part of it has been again several days without Bread—and for the rest we have not either on the spot or within reach a supply sufficient for four days—Nor does this deficiency proceed from accidental obstructions as has been the case on former occasions but from the absolute emptiness of our magazines every where and the total want of money or credit to replenish them. I look forward to the consequences with an anxiety not to be described."

As an expedient, the American commander proposed a loan of five thousand barrels of flour out of the stores set aside for the use of the French fleet and army. "If this can be obtained to be replaced as spe[e]dily as possible, perhaps it may prove a timely relief; the mean while we shall do every thing in our power to husband the little stock we have and draw all the aid the surrounding Country can afford—I know the measure recommended is a disagreeable one; but motives of delicacy must often yield to those of necessity; and in the present case it appears to me to admit not of hesitation."[7]

The dangerous situation at the end of the year prompted him to seek aid from the states. He issued a circular letter to the state executives on December 16. "The situation of the Army with respect to supplies is beyond description alarming," he advised them,

It has been five or six Weeks past on half allowance, and we have not three days Bread or a third allowance on hand nor any where within reach. When this is exhausted we must depend on the precarious gleanings of the neighbouring country. Our Magazines are absolutely empty every where and our Commissaries intirely destitute of money or credit to replenish them. We have never experienced a like extremity at any period of the War. We have often felt temporary want from accidental delays in forwarding supplies; but we always had something in our Magazines and the means of procuring more. Neither one nor the other is at present the case. This representation is the result of a minute examination of our resources. Unless some extraordinary exertions be made by the States from which we draw our supplies there is every appearance that the Army will infallibly disband in a fortnight.

Washington asked for "the vigorous interposition" of the states "to rescue us from the danger of an event, which if it did not prove the total ruin of our affairs, would at least give them a shock from which they would not easily recover, and plunge us into a train of new and still more perplexing embarrassments than any we have hitherto felt."[8]

Expressing his "Mortification" at the situation of the army, New Jersey governor William Livingston replied that "To find our Troops in want of Bread at the close of so glorious a Campaign; & to think of administring such cause of triumph & Exultation to the Enemy, & of Disgrace & Astonishment to all Europe, requires no uncommon fortitude to bear with any tolerable patience." But he had "anticipated the dreadful Event." He then went on to propose a plan for a remedy, a plan later adopted by Congress (and which proved equally as ineffective as the current system):

It is not my Disposition Sir to excuse myself from any trouble by which I can render my Country essential Service (whether in the immediate line of my Department or out of it) by a fruitless crimination of others; which tho' it may ease the Stomach of the Satyrist by discharging his resentment, will not fill those of the Soldiery with Food. It is not by reproaching others, but by the most vigorous Exertions of our own, that we can now hope to feed, a meritorious, & too much-neglected Army. But notwithstanding this, every virtuous Citizen of America will think himself entitled to complain when after issuing in about twenty months . . . to the Departments of the Commissary & Quarte[r] Master General above one hundred & thirty millions of Dollars, we are in the most perillous Predicament, & the Army on the Point of disbanding for the want of Supplies. . . . I have seen the meanest officers in those Departments growing rich, without any other conceiveable means than by those of Fraud & peculation. It is therefore become indispensible, & absolutely so, to put those purchases into the hands of the respective States where the Supplies are furnished, to request their management of them, & to apply the Taxes raised, to this Effect, or such part however as may be necessary.

For the immediate relief of the army he promised Washington that he would urge the legislature of his state "to adopt by resolve more vigorous Measures" to supply the troops. Leading members of the legislature had promised him "to exert every nerve in providing the most speedy & effectual remedy for our present Distress."[9]

After receiving the circular, Joseph Reed, president of the Supreme Executive Council of Pennsylvania, wrote to Washington: "We did not consider it wise or prudent to spend Time in unavailing Complaints of Misman[a]gement or Neglect but to endeavour to apply a Remedy." The council, he reported, after inquiring about the amount of flour in the Philadelphia area, "found a greater Supply than at first we expected; the whole amounting to 2500 Barrlls which might be spared, of all which we gave immediate Notice to Congress pointing out the Places where it lay & offering our utmost Aid & Assistance in procuring it." Additional inquiries had resulted in locating "some Quantities of Wheat in the Brandywine & other Mills which with Attenti[o]n may be procured for publick Purposes." But he advised the general that crops in the state were not as plentiful as previously believed. The supply of the French fleet and sending flour to Maryland had reduced what was available. Pennsylvania had also supplied a great number of rations to the army. Philadelphia alone, he explained, had provided 9,400 rations in the past summer alone. "This heavy Consumpti[o]n must necessarily exhaust our Resources & prevent our giving that Aid which might otherwise be expected. However your Excelly may be assured that nothing shall be wanting on our Part to give the necessary Relief whatever we may think of the Causes of such a Calamity. The Assembly will meet in a short Time, Taxes are in vigorous Collecti[o]n throughout this State—& if some fatal unforeseen Influence does not blast our Prospects we think a similar Scene will never present itself."[10]

Replies from other governors were equally noncommittal or only held out promises of future action. George Clinton, governor of New York, advised Washington that immediately after receiving the circular he had convened the state's purchasing commissaries to determine what supplies they could furnish "and whether any Exertions of mine would tend to forward the Business of their Department on this pressing Occasion." But after the "minutest Inquiry" he had discovered "that we shall not have it in our Power to do more than supply the present Garrison of Fort Schuyler & the Posts in the Highlands with the Troops in their Vicinity computing the daily Issues at 40 Barrels of Flour." Prior assessments of wheat by the legislature on the state's farmers had barely furnished a daily supply for the troops in the state and he doubted if the latest assessment could be collected, manufactured into flour, and delivered to Fishkill, New York, before "the Troops in this Quarter will suffer." The present depreciated state of the currency would, he feared, prevent the commissaries "from doing any Thing effectually . . . besides the want of Cash in the Hands of the Persons employed to purchase, the exorbitant Prices which our Farmers hear are given in some of the Southern States occasions so great an unwillingness in them to dispose of their Produce at any Rate that I apprehend very little (other than what is forced from them by the Authority of Law) will be procured." But, he advised, "if these Difficulties were removed and a Proportion of Indian Corn & Rye was manufactured with the Wheat into Flour for immediate Use, it would so lengthen out the Supplies which may be procured in this State as to enable us, to do much more towards feeding the Army—The Bread will certainly be equally wholesome & nourishing for the Troops; But without this (if the last Crops in the other States have been equally injured) a real Scarcity with the fatal Consequences which will attend it is to be apprehended."[11] The governor of Maryland replied that his legislature had determined "to make the most Vigorous Exertions in sending forward every Supply the State is capable of furnishing."[12]

But despite all such promises, large stocks of provisions sufficient to meet the army's needs failed to arrive.

Shortly after the new year, and in the midst of severe winter weather, the lack of food provisions became so extreme that Washington implemented a "requisition" on the counties of New Jersey (the bulk of the army was camped in that state near Morristown). He announced his decision in a circular to the New Jersey county magistrates that made it clear that compliance could be voluntary but, if not, would be forced. "Gentlemen," he wrote,

> the present situation of the army with respect to provisions is the most distressing of any we have experienced since the beginning of the war. For a fortnight past the troops, both officers and men, have been almost perishing for want. They have been alternately without bread or meat; the whole time with a very scanty allowance of either, and frequently destitute of both. They have borne their sufferings with a patience that merits the approbation, and ought to excite the sympathy of their countrymen. But they are now reduced to an extremity no longer to be supported. The distress has in some instances prompted the men to commit depredations on the property of the inhabitants, which at any other period would be punished with examplary severity, but which can now only be lamented as the effect of an unfortunate necessity. This evil would increase, and soon become intolerable were not an instant remedy to be applied.
>
> The distress we feel is chiefly owing to the early commencement and uncommon rigor of the winter, which have greatly obstructed the transportation of our supplies. These causes have obliged us to exhaust all the magazines in the vicinity of camp, and as they continue to operate we shall be unable to derive seasonable sucour from our more distant resources. From present appearances it

must be four or five weeks before we can have the benefit of any material supplies beyond the limits of this State, so that unless an extraordinary exertion be made within the State to supply the wants of the army during that space fatal consequences must unavoidably ensue. Your own discernment makes it needless to particularize.

Influenced by these considerations my duty to the public, and my affection to the virtuous inhabitants of this State (who next to the army would be the most immediate sufferers) have determined me to call upon the respective counties for a proportion of grain and cattle to satisfy the present exigency. . . . I have adopted this mode of application, from a regard to the ease and accommodation of the inhabitants. As you are well acquainted with the circumstances of individuals you will be able to apportion the quantity required to the ability of each, and as I have no doubt you will be convinced of the absolute necessity of the measure, I am persuaded your zeal for the common cause will induce you to exert your utmost influence to procure a cheerful and immediate compliance. In doing this though you may not be authorized by the strict letter of the law, by consulting its spirit (which aims at the relief of the army) in an emergency of so pressing and peculiar a nature, you will merit the acknowlegements of your fellow citizens.

He promised that the inhabitants would receive "certificates specifying the quantity of each article and the terms of payment" at present market price or the market price at the time of payment.[13] "While I have entire confidence that you will do every thing in your power to give efficacy to this requisition," he continued, "I have too high an opinion of the patriotism of the p[e]ople of this State and of their attatchment to an army making every sacrifice in defence of their country, to entertain the least apprehension of their not seconding your endeavours. But at the same time I think it my duty to inform you, that should we be disappointed in our hopes, the extremity of the case will compel us to have recourse to a different mode which will be disagreeable to me on every account; on none more than the probability of its having an operation less equal and less convenient to the inhabitants than the one now recommended." Reminding them that the army could expect no relief "through the ordinary channels," the general declared that "you will be sensible that delay or indecision is incompatable with our circumstances."[14]

Washington usually deplored such a threat of force against citizens. That he used it in this case shows his desperation to supply the army. His letter to the field officers assigned to supervise the "requisition" made clear the nature of the compulsion to be used, if necessary: "The present distresses of the Army with which you are well acquainted, have determined me to call upon the respective Counties of the State for a proportion of Grain and Cattle according to the abilities of each. For this purpose I have addressed the Magistrates of every County to induce them to undertake the business. This mode I have preferred as the one least inconvenient to the Inhabitants; but in case the requisition should not be complied with, we must then raise the supplies ourselves in the best manner we can."

Giving each officer the type and amount of provisions expected from his assigned county, Washington directed that each officer proceed to their county

with all dispatch, and, calling upon the Justices, will deliver them the inclosed Address, enforcing it with a more particular detail of the sufferings of the Troops the better to convince them of the necessity of their exertions. You will at the same time delicately let them know, that you are instructed, in case they do not take up the business immediately, to begin to impress the Articles called for, throughout the Country. You will press for an immediate Answer and govern yourself accordingly. If it be a compliance, you will concert with them a proper place for the reception of the Articles; and the time of delivery, which for the whole is to be in Four days after your application to them. . . . In case of refusal you will begin to impress till you make up the quantity required. This you will do with as much tenderness as possible to the Inhabitants, having regard to the Stock of each Individual, that no family may be deprived of its necessary subsistence. . . . You are also authorised to impress Waggons for the transportation of the Grain. . . .

I have reposed this trust in You from a perfect confidence in your prudence, zeal and respect for the rights of Citizens. While your measures are adapted to the emergency—and you consult what you owe to the service—I am persuaded you will not forget; that as we are compelled by necessity to take the property of Citizens for the support of the Army on whom their safety depends, we should be careful to manifest that we have a reverence for their rights, and wish not to do any thing which that necessity and even their own good do not absolutely require.[15]

As with his other appeals for aid, this "requisition" on New Jersey, though successful, managed to provide only temporary relief to the army. Lack of provisions continued to haunt the army throughout 1780.

Washington began the year facing difficulties in clothing the army. In an early memorandum to the committee of conference, he wrote: "The Cloathing department appears to be altogether unsettled and confused and requires immediate attention. . . . The army is now greatly deficient in the articles of blankets and hats, and shoes, or soon will be, as these last are in constant demand."[16]

In the later part of January, the general addressed the clothing issue in detail. "Cloathing the Army well is a matter of such essential and fundamental importance, that it ought not by any means to depend on contingencies, but some plan should if possible be concerted to produce regular and constant Supplies," he wrote to the committee. Washington then laid out such a plan. His detailed proposal covered every consideration. Several excerpts from the document will suffice to show the comprehensive nature of the report: "The united funds and Credit of the Continent appears to me the only sufficient Basis for the extensive supplies which are required," he wrote:

Any other it is to be feared would be too contracted and render them too precarious. . . . If governmental Contracts can be made as suggested in the first case, they will put the matter upon a more certain footing than can be done in any other way . . . as it will be some time before the necessary provision can be made upon either of the two first plans, it will be proper to call upon each State in the most pressing manner to make every exertion for supplying its own troops. . . . In order to be certain of obtaining competent Supplies, much larger quantities than are really wanted ought to be sent for, and every Cargo properly assorted. . . . With a view to this, that more of the materials may not be made up than are wanted and the better to fit the cloathing to the Men, as every Regiment I believe has Taylors enough to make up its own, I would recommend that Materials for Cloathing rather than Cloathes ready made be imported. . . . The Clothier General in the first instance will be necessary to furnish Estimates of the Supplies wanted for the Army—to receive those supplies—superintend the distribution of them to the State Clothiers—make these account for what they receive at stated periods . . . to stand as it were between the public and the Army, seeing that the first is not imposed on and that the last gets whatever is allowed in a regular, direct and seasonable manner. . . . The Sub or State Clothier should be appointed by his own State (especially if each State is to provide for its own troops). If the Army is supplied on Continental account—he will receive the proportion of Cloathing for the troops of the State to which he belongs from the Clothier General, which he will issue to the Regimental Clothiers. . . . In Case the States should each provide for its own troops—the Sub or State Clothier who should always reside with or near the Army to know and supply the wants of the troops the better, is to call upon the Governor or purchasing Agent of the State for the Supplies wanted from time to time.

To prevent in future any unequal distribution of Cloathing either to the Regiments or Officers, and the confusion and loss which have heretofore been occasioned, and would for ever be occasioned by having no regular plan for issuing it, and to check irregular applications from commanding Officers of Regiments to public Agents in different parts—it ought to be strictly enjoined on those Agents—on the Clothier Genl and on the Sub or State Clothiers, to issue no Cloathing but through the Channels already pointed out. . . . I beg leave to give it as my opinion, that if Congress by a decisive Act of theirs would point out the Colour of the Cloth for each State, and the Uniform of each Regiment and adhere to it invariably, the following good consequences . . . would result—First it would prevent in case of State purchases an interference . . . because the Colour of one State would not suit that of another—Secondly by having many Colours you do not increase the demand and of course the price of any one. Thirdly, it is a great advantage to have one Corps distinguished from another, because the good and bad deeds of the Soldiers—honorable and dishonorable Actions of the Officers are easier brought to light, the Uniform being a ready index to discoveries of this kind—And lastly, Officers by becoming acquainted with the fixed Uniform of their State and Regiment, and knowing that it is not to be changed as fancy and the caprice of a commanding Officer may direct, can take measures accordingly and avoid running into the unnecessary expence and trouble occasioned by the discretionary changes which happen.[17]

Lack of action in Congress on his proposal prompted Washington to address that body on the issue of clothing in March:

When an important matter is suspended for deliberation in Congress, I should be sorry that my sollicitude to have it determined, should contribute to a premature decision. But when I have such striking proofs of public loss & private discontent from the present management of the clothing department—when accts, inadmissible if any system existed, frequently remind me of the absolute necessity of introducing one—When I hear as I often do, of large importations of cloathing which we never see—of quantities wasting and rotting in different parts of the Country, the knowledge of which reaches me by chance—When I have reason to believe that the money which has been expended for cloathing the Army, if judiciously laid out, & the Cloaths regularly issued, would have effectually answered the purpose—And when I have never till now seen it other wise than half naked. When I feel the perplexity and additional load of business thrown upon me by the irregularity in this department—and by applications from all parts of the Army for relief—I cannot forbear discovering my anxiety to have some plan decided for conducting the business hereafter, in a more provident & consistent manner. If the one I proposed to the Committee does not coincide with the Sentiments of Congress, I should be happy some other could be substituted.[18]

Congress eventually adopted parts of Washington's plan, but problems with clothing persisted at the end of the year. Washington wrote clothier general James Wilkinson in December: "From the wretched & miserable condition of many of the Troops for want of their Cloathes, Many of them being absolutely naked, I must urge again in the most earnest terms, that you will use every possible & Instant exertion to have the Cloathing as formerly directed, brought forward that it may be delivered. The public service as well as the dictates of humanity require that it should be done without a moment's delay. That there may not be any impediments on the score of transportation—You will apply to the Quarter Master Genl & inform him it [is] my desire that every practicable exertion should be made to get the Cloathing down."[19]

Clothing the army required transportation to move the material to camp. The shortage of wagons induced Washington to address Maj. Gen. Nathanael Greene, quartermaster general of the army, the day after writing the clothier general: "The distress of a great part of the troops for want of Cloathing, particularly in the essential article of shoes, which would render them useless, should circumstances require the activity of the army, induces me to request your exertions to give the Clothier the assistance he may stand in need of for bringing on his supplies—These have been delayed much longer than I expected for want of the means of transportation; and it is certainly of very great importance in the present posture of things that we should have it in our power to avail ourselves of the whole of our small force on an emergency."[20]

Washington's efforts resulted, as with so many issues of administration and supply he faced, in only temporary relief of his soldiers. The lack of adequate clothing persisted into 1780.

As with clothing, Washington began the year discussing the need to increase the strength of the army's regiments. In an early memorandum to the committee of conference, he had proposed drafting soldiers and he again addressed recruiting in a letter to the committee five days later.[21] But by March, Congress had taken no action on his suggestions, and he felt compelled to address the issue with that body. The letter, which I quote here nearly in full, shows not only the general's need for more men but his grasp of the state of affairs in Great Britain and the military situation throughout the continent:

> I have waited with anxious expectations, for some plan to be adopted by Congress which would have a general operation throughout the States for compleating their respective Battalions. No plan for this purpose has yet come to my knowledge, nor do I find that the several Governments are pursuing any measures to accomplish the end by particular arrangements of their own legislatures. I therefore hope Congress will excuse any appearance of importunity, in my troubling them again on the subject, as I earnestly wish to be enabled to realize some ideas on what may be expected towards the completion of our Batalions by the opening of the next campaign. They are already greatly reduced, and will be much more so by that time; owing to the expiration of the term of Service of the last years drafts.
>
> At the Posts in the highlands, Nixons, Pattersons and Learneds Brigades alone, will suffer (by the first of April) a diminution of 847 Men, which must be replaced, illy as they can, and reluctantly as they will be spared from other Posts. . . .
>
> Among the Troops of some States, recruiting in Camp on the new bounties has succeeded tolerably well; among others, where the expectations of state bounties have had more influence, very ill; Upon the whole, the success has been far short of our wishes and will probably be so of our necessities.
>
> The measure of inlisting in the Country, in my opinion depends so much on the abolishing of State bounties, that without it, I am doubtful whether it will be worth the experiment. State bounties, have been a source of immense expence and many misfortunes.

The sooner the practice can be abolished, and system introduced in our manner of recruiting and keeping up our batalions, as well as in the administration of the several departments of the Army, the sooner will our Security be established and placed out of the reach of contingencies. Temporary expedients to serve the purposes of the moment, occasion more difficulties and expence, than can easily be conceived.

The superior information, which Congress may have, of the political state of affairs in Europe and of combining circumstances may induce them to believe that, there will soon be a termination of the War; and therefore, that the expence of vigorous measures to re-inforce the Army may be avoided. If this should be the case, I dare say the reasons will be well considered before a plan is adopted; which, whatever advantages of oeconomy it may promise, in an eventual disappointment, may be productive of ruinous consequences. For my own part, I confess I should be cautious of admitting the supposition that the War will terminate without another desperate effort on the part of the enemy.

The Speech of the Prince, and the debates of his Ministers have very little the aspect of peace; and if we reflect, that they are subsequent (as I apprehend they must have been) to the events, on which our hopes appear to be founded, they must seem no bad argumts. of a determination in the British cabinet to continue the War. Tis true, whether this be the determination or not, tis a very natural policy that every exertion should be made by them to be in the best condition to oppose thier enemies, and that there should be every appearance of vigor and preparation. But if the Ministry had serious thoughts of making peace, they would hardly insist so much as they do, on the particular point of prosecuting the American War. They would not like to raise and inflame the expectations of the People on this subject, while it was secretly their intention to disappoint them. In America, every thing has the complexion of a continuance of the War. The operations of the enemy in the Southern States do not resemble a transient incursion, but a serious conquest. At their posts in this quarter, every thing is in a state of tranquility, and indicates a design, at least, to hold possession. These considerations joined to the preceeding. The infinite pains that are taken to keep up the Spirits of the [Loyalists] and to assure them of support and protection; and several other circumstances, trifling in themselves but powerful when combined, amount to no contemptable evidence that the contest is not so near an end, as we could wish. I am fully sensible of many weighty reasons on the opposite side; but I do not think them sufficiently conclusive to destroy the force of what has been suggested, or to justify the sanguine inferences many seem inclined to draw.

Should the Court of Britain be able to send any reinforcements to America the next campaign, and carry on offensive operations; and should we not take some effectual means to recruit our batalions. When we shall have detached the force necessary to act decisively against the Indians, and the remaining drafts shall have returned home; the force which remains for our defence will be very inconsiderable indeed. We must then on every exigency have recourse to the Militia, the consequence of which, besides weakness and defeat in the field, will be double or treble the necessary expence to the public. To say nothing of the injury to agriculture which attends calling out the Militia on particular emergencies and at some critical Seasons, they are commonly twice as long coming to where they are wanted and returning home, as they are in the field; and must of course for every days real service receive two or three days pay, and consume the same proportion of provisions.[22]

The states seemed to Washington to want to rely on militia and so were reluctant to provide sufficient recruits to bring their Continental regiments up to strength. As he hinted in the previous letter, he put no stock in militia as a field force. He deplored the position this stance of the states, and those in Congress who supported that view, forced his army to endure. Also, even with this attitude, governors called on him to station Continental troops in their states—something his low number of troops would not allow even if it made strategic sense (which it often did not).

In a private letter to a friend and member of Congress in May, Washington explained this difficult situation:

As a variety of accidents may disappoint our hopes here, it is indispensable we should make every exertion on our part to check the enemy's progress. This cannot be done to effect, if our reliance is solely or principally on militia; for a force continually fluctuating is incapable of any material effort. The states concerned ought by all means to endeavour to draw out men for a length of time; a smaller number on this plan would answer their purpose better; a great deal of expence would be avoided and agriculture would be much less impeded. It is to be lamented that the remoteness and weakness of this army, would make it folly to attempt to send any succour from this quarter. Perhaps for want of knowing the true state of our foreign expectations and prospects of finance, I may be led to contemplate the gloomy side of things—But I confess they appear to me to be in a very disagreeable train—The rapid decay of our currency, the extinction of public spirit—the increasing rapacity of the times, the want of harmony in our councils—the declining zeal of the people—the discontents and distresses of the officers of the army—and I may add the prevailing security and insensibility to danger—are symptoms in my eye of a most alarming nature—If the Enemy have it in their power to press us hard this campaign I know not what may be the consequence. Our army as it now stands is little more than the skeleton of an army—& I hear of no steps that are taking to give it strength and substance—I hope there may not be great mistakes on this head, and that our abilities in general are not overrated—The applications for succour are numerous; but no pains are taken to put it in my power to afford them. When I endeavour to draw together the Continental troops for the most essential purposes I am embarrassed with complaints of the exhausted defenceless situation of particular states and find myself obliged either to resist solicitations made in such a manner and with such a degree of emphasis as scarcely to leave me a choice, or to sacrifice the most obvious principles of military propriety and risk the general safety.[23]

His continuing need for troops for the campaign prompted
Washington to issue a circular letter to the state executives in May.
In it, he set out the full situation of the army and the country. It was
an effort to rouse the state governments to action. "The state of the
army in particular is alarming on several accounts," he explained,

that of its numbers is not among the least. Our battalions are exceedingly reduced, not only from the natural decay incident to the
best composed armies; but from the expiration of the term of service for which a large proportion of the men were engaged. The
measures hitherto taken to replace them, so far as has come to my
knowledge have been attended with very partial success; and I am
ignorant of any others in contemplation that afford a better
prospect. A reinforcement expected from Virginia, consisting of
new levies and reinlisted men is necessarily ordered to the Southward. Not far short of one third of our whole force must be detached on a service undertaken by the direction of Congress,[24] and
essential in itself. I shall only say of what remains, that when it is
compared with the force of the enemy now actually at new York
and Rhode Island, with the addition of the succours, they will in
all proba[bi]lity receive from England, at the lowest computa-
tion—it will be found to justify very serious apprehensions and to
demand the zealous attention of the different legislatures.

When we consider the rapid decline of our currency—the general temper of the times the disaffection of a great part of the people—the lethargy that overspreads the rest—the increasing danger
to the Southern States—we cannot but dread the consequences of
any misfortune in this quarter; and must feel the impolicy of trusting our security—to a want of activity and enterprise in the enemy.

An expectation of peace and an opinion of the enemy's inability
to send more troops to this country, I fear, have had too powerful
an influence in our affairs. I have never heard any thing conclusive
to authorise the former, and present appearances are in my opinion against it. The accounts we receive from Europe uniformly announce vigorous preparations to continue the war at least another
campaign. The debates and proceedings in parliament wear this

complexion. The public papers speak confidently of large reinforcements destined for America.

He concluded by writing, "These considerations and many more
that might be suggested point to the necessity of immediate and
decisive exertions to complete our battalions and to make our
military force more respectable. I thought it my duty to give an idea
of its true state and to urge the attention of the States to a matter in
which their safety and happiness are so deeply interested."[25]

The situation had not improved in the summer, although
temporary drafts promised some additions to the army's strength.
Washington wrote in July to the Continental commander in South
Carolina:

> I sincerely sympathise with you my Dr Sr, in the disagreeable
> aspect of our affairs to the Southward, and in the embarrassments
> to which your situation must necessarily expose you—Had it been
> possible to have afforded you any succours from the army under
> my command; you may be assured that public and personal mo-
> tives would have equally induced me to do it—But you are not
> unacquainted with the insufficiency of our means every where,
> and the States in general seem to have been for some time past in
> a profound sleep. They have been amusing themselves with idle
> dreams of peace, and have scarcely made any exertions for the
> war. Till within a fortnight this army has scarcely received a single
> recruit, though a large part of it dissolved in the course of the last
> winter and spring by the expiration of the term of service for
> which the men were engaged—We have now a prospect of a thou-
> sand or fifteen hundred levies, at enormous bounties, for nine
> months from the States of Massachusetts & Connecticut which
> make up our whole expectations of reinforcement. Inferior in
> strength to the enemy we are able to do little more than to take
> care of ourselves and guard the communication of this river [the
> Hudson], which is supposed to be a main object of Sir Harry Clin-
> tons operations, and is certainly the point in which we are most
> essentially vulnerable.[26]

And to Joseph Reed he wrote in August: "No Man dislikes short and temporary enlistments more than I do—No man ever had greater cause to reprobate and even curse the fatal policy of the measure than I have—nor no man (with decency) ever opposed it more in the early part of this contes," he asserted. Had his advice on this matter been acted on in 1775 and 1776, he argued, the Continental currency would have "been upon a very different establishment in point of credit." Millions in bounty money to enlistees would have been saved, as well as "the consequent evils of expiring armies, and new levies. But those hours are passed never to be recalled." The bulk of the enlisted men now in the army, he believed, were "in a different train of thinking and acting to what they were in the early stages of the war." Nothing was now left to maintain the army "but an annual & systematical mode of drafting; which while we retain the stamina of an army (engaged for the War) will be the best, indeed I see no other substitute, for voluntary enlistment." He wondered, though, how those state "governments wch are rent & weakened by intestine divisions" would "have energy enough to carry Statutes of this nature into execution." But he felt "such as are well established & organized, I am sure can do it." And even with those that were not "the propriety of the measure is so necessary and obvious, that I should entertain little doubt of their success in the experiment."[27]

These temporary drafts and calls for militia enabled Washington to contemplate and prepare for a major offensive in the fall (see chapter 4), but when their time of service expired the following winter he was reduced to the same situation. His struggle to recruit the strength of the army would also continue in 1780.

In 1779, Washington wrote several private letters to trusted friends that set out his candid views of the country's situation. These letters reveal insights about his attitude regarding the state of the nation rarely conveyed in his public letters. Because they are so revealing, they deserve extensive quotation. In a two-part letter of December 1778, penned just before and just after his journey to Philadelphia to confer with a committee of Congress (see chapter 1), he laid out

his views to his friend Benjamin Harrison. The letter is one of the
most revealing ever written by Washington. "I can assign but two
causes for the enemys continuance among us," he wrote,

and these balance so equally in my Mind, that I scarce know
which of the two preponderates. The one is, that they are waiting
the ultimate determination of Parliament; the other, that of our
distresses; by which I know the Commissioners went home not a
little buoyed up; and sorry I am to add, not without cause. What
may be the effect of such large and frequent emissions, of the dissentions, Parties, extravigance, and a general lax of public virtue
Heaven alone can tell! I am affraid even to think of It; but it appears as clear to me as ever the Sun did in its meredian brightness,
that America never Stood in more eminent need of the wise, patriotic, and Spirited exertions of her Sons than at this period and
if it is not a sufficient cause for genl. lamentation, my misconcep-
tion of the matter impresses it too strongly upon me, that the
States seperately are too much engaged in their local concerns,
and have too many of their ablest men withdrawn from the general Council for the good of the common weal; in a word, I think
our political system may, be compared to the mechanism of a
Clock; and that our conduct should derive a lesson from it for it
answers no good purpose to keep the smaller Wheels in order if
the greater one which is the support and prime mover of the whole
is neglected. How far the latter is the case does not become me to
pronounce but as their can be no harm in a pious wish for the
good of ones Country I shall offer it as mine that each State wd
not only choose, but absolutely compel their ablest Men to attend
Congress; that they would instruct them to go into a thorough in-
vestigation of the causes that have produced so many disagreeable
effects in the Army and Country; in a word that public abuses
should be corrected, and an entire reformation worked; without
these it does not, in my judgment, require the spirit of divination
to foretell the consequences of the present Administration, nor to
how little purpose the States, individually, are framing constitu-
tions, providing laws, and filling Offices with the abilities of their
ablest Men. These, if the great whole is mismanaged must sink in

the general wreck and will carry with it the remorse of thinking
that we are lost by our own folly and negligence, or the desire perhaps of living in ease and tranquility during the expected accom-
plishment of so great a revolution in the effecting of which the
greatest abilities and the honestest Men our (i.e. the American)
world affords ought to be employed. It is much to be feared my
dear Sir that the States in their seperate capacities have very inadequate ideas of the present danger. Removed (some of them) far
distant from the scene of action and seeing, and hearing such publications only as flatter their wishes they conceive that the contest
is at an end, and that to regulate the government and police of
their own State is all that remains to be done; but it is devoutly to
be wished that a sad reverse of this may not fall upon them like a
thunder clap that is little expected. I do not mean to designate particular States. I wish to cast no reflections upon any one. The Public believes (and if they do believe it, the fact might almost as well
be so) that the States at this time are badly represented, and that
the great, and important concerns of the nation are horribly conducted, for want either of abilities or application in the Members,
or through discord and party views of some individuals; that they
should be so, is to be lamented more at this time, than formerly,
as we are far advanced in the dispute and in the opinn. of many
drawg. to a happy period; have the eyes of Europe upon us, and
I am perswaded many political Spies to watch, discover our situation, and give information of our weaknesses and wants.

Washington added a postscript after completing his journey and
having his first meetings with the committee of conference: "This
Letter was to have gone by Post from Middle brook but missed that
conveyance, since which I have come to this place at the request of
Congress whence I shall soon return," he advised Harrison. "I have
seen nothing since I came here (on the 22d. [of December]) to change
my opinion of Men or Measrs. but abundant reason to be convinced,
that our Affairs are in a more distressed, ruinous, and deplorable
condition than they have been in Since the commencement of the
War." He continued:

By a faithful labourer then in the cause. By a Man who is daily injuring his private Estate without even the smallest earthly advantage not common to all in case of a favourable Issue to the dispute. By one who wishes the prosperity of America most devoutly and sees or thinks he sees it, on the brink of ruin, you are beseeched most earnestly my dear Colo. Harrison to exert yourself in endeavouring to rescue your Country, by, (let me add) sending your ablest and best Men to Congress. These characters must not slumber, nor sleep at home, in such times of pressing danger; they must not content themselves in the enjoyment of places of honor or profit in their own Country, while the common interests of America are mouldering and sinking into irretrievable (if a remedy is not soon applied) ruin, in which theirs also must ultimately be involved. If I was to be called upon to draw A picture of the times, and of Men, from what I have Seen, heard, and in part know I should in one word say that idleness, dissipation and extravagance seems to have laid fast hold of most of them. That Speculation, peculation, and an insatiable thirst for riches seems to have got the better of every other consideration and almost of every order of Men. That party disputes and personal quarrels are the great business of the day whilst the momentous concerns of an empire, a great and accumulated debt; ruined finances, depreciated money, and want of credit (which in their consequences is the want of every thing) are but secondary considerations and postponed from day to day, from week to week as if our affairs wore the most promising aspect. after drawing this picture, which from my Soul I believe to be a true one I need not repeat to you that I am alarmed and wish to see my Countrymen roused. I have no resentments, nor do I mean to point at any particular characters; this I can declare upon my honor for I have every attention paid me by Congress that I can possibly expect and have reason to think that I stand well in their estimation but in the present situation of things I cannot help asking: Where is Mason, Wythe, Jefferson, Nicholas, Pendleton, Nelson, and another I could name; and why, if you are sufficiently impressed with your danger, do you not (as New Yk. has done in the case of Mr Jay) send an extra Member or two for at least a certain limited time till the great business of the Nation is put upon a more respectable and happy establishmt. Your Money is now sinking 5 pr. Ct. a day in this City; and I shall not be surprized if in the course of a few months a total stop is put to the currency of it. And yet an assembly, a concert, a Dinner, or Supper (that will cost three or four hundred pounds) will not only take Men from acting in but even from thinking of this business while a great part of the Officers of your Army from absolute necessity are quitting the Service and the more virtuous few rather than do this are sinking by sure degrees into beggery and want. I again repeat to you that this is not an exagerated acct.; that it is an alarming one I do not deny, and confess to you that I feel more real distress on acct. of the prest. appearances of things than I have done at any one time since the commencement of the dispute. But it is time to bid you, once more adieu. Providence has heretofore taken us up when all other means and hope seemed to be departing from us, in this I will confide.[28]

When Washington wrote again to Harrison in May his outlook had changed little. "If my time would permit, and it was proper and safe by the Post to go into a free discussion of the political state of our affairs I could, and would, write you a very long letter on this subject," he wrote,

but this kind of conveyance is too uncertain (while the enemy are pursuing with avidity every means in their power to come at the sentiments of men in office) to hazard such opinions as I could wish to convey; I shall only remark therefore, that no day passes without some proofs of the justness of the observations contained in My letter to you [of December 18] and the necessity of the measure there recommended; if it is much longer neglected I shall not scruple to add, that our affairs are irretrievably lost! I see no cause to retract a single sentiment contained in that long letter, but many very many, alarming proofs in confirmation of the truth of them. if the letter therefore is in being you are possessed as fully of my ideas on the several matters there touched as I have words to express them, and may allow them such weight as you think they deserve. An instance in proof of one of my positions I may give, because it is a fact of such notariety that to the enemy, and to ourselves, it is equally well known; it is, that Beef in the Market of Phila. is from ten to 15*l*. a pound, and other things in proportion. Country produce and imported Goods are equally dear; under these circumstances, and no appearances that I can see of a radical cure, it is not difficult to predict the fate of our Paper Money, and with it, a general Crash of all things.

The measures of Ministry are taken; and the whole strength and resources of the Kingdom will be exerted against us this Campaign; while we have been either slumbering and sleeping or disputing upon trifles, contenting ourselves with laughing at the impotence of G. Britain which we supposed to be on her knees begging mercy of us, and forgiveness for past offences, instead of devising ways and means to recruit our Battalions, provide supplies, and improving our finances, thereby providing against the worst & a very possible contingency.

Accts. from Londn. to the 9th. of March have fixed me in the opinion that G. Britain will strain every nerve to distress us this Campaign but where, or in what manner her principal force will be employed I cannot determine; that a pretty considerable number of Troops will be sent from G. Britain does not, I think, admit of a doubt; but whether for the West Indies, Georgia, or New York, or partly to all three, time must unfold; my own opinion of the matter is, that they will keep a respectable force at the last mentioned place and push their operations vigorously to the Southward where we are most vulnerable and least able to afford succour.

By extracts from English Papers of the 4th. of March it appears pretty evident that Seven Regiments, besides two of the New raised Scotch Corps, Recruits for the Guards, and other Regits. now in America, were upon the point of embarking, the whole it is said would amount to 12 or 13000 Men. A Bill has passed both Houses of Parliament obliging each parish in the Kingdom to furnish two Men by which it is said 27,000 will be raised. With this augmn. and her fleets, which are more than a match for the Naval strength of France alone, she may, circumstanced as we are, give a very unfavourable turn to that pleasing Slumber we have been in for the last eight Months and which has produced nothing but dreams of Peace and Independance, if Spain can be kept quiet; to effect which there is no doubt but that all the Art and address of the Ministry will be displayed and with too much success it is to be feared, as it will be difficult upon any political ground (I am capable of investigating) to acct. for the backwardness of that Court if it means to take an active part; as the Fleets of France and Independance of America are hazarded by the delay.

From present appearances, I have not the smallest doubt but that we shall be hard pushed in every quarter. This campaign will be the grand, and if unsuccessful, more than probably the last struggle of G. Britain; how much then does it behoove us to be prepar'd at all points to avert their intended blows.[29]

In March, with the army still in camp at Middlebrook, New Jersey, Washington wrote to his friend from Virginia, George Mason: "Though it is not in my power to devote much time to private correspondences, owing to the multiplicity of public letters (and other business) I have to read, write, & transact; yet I can with great truth assure you, that it would afford me very singular pleasure to be favoured at all times with your sentiments in a leizure hour, upon public matters of general concernment as well as those which more immediately respect yr. own State (if proper conveyance wd. render prudent a free communication)."

"I am particularly desirous of it at this time," he continued,

because I view things very differently, I fear, from what people in general do who seem to think the contest is at an end; and to make money, and get places, the only things now remaining to do. I have seen without dispondency (even for a moment) the hours which America have stiled her gloomy ones, but I have beheld no day since the commencement of hostilities that I have thought her liberties in such emiment danger as at present. Friends and foes seem now to combine to pull down the goodly fabric we have hitherto been raising at the expence of so much time, blood, and treasure—

and unless the bodies politick will exert themselves to bring things back to first principles—correct abuses—& punish our internal foes, inevitable ruin must follow. Indeed we seem to be verging so fast to destruction, that I am filled with sensations to which I have been a stranger till within these three Months. Our Enemys beholds with exultation & joy how effectually we labour for their benefit; & from being in a state of absolute dispair, & on the point of evacuating America, are now on tiptoe—nothing therefore in my judgment can save us but a total reformation in our own conduct, or some decisive turn to affairs in Europe. The former alas! to our shame be it spoken! is less likely to happen than the latter, as it is now consistent with the views of the Speculators—variant tribes of money makers—& stock jobbers of all denominations to continue the War for their own private emolument, with out considering that their avarice, & thirst for gain must plunge every thing (including themselves) in one common Ruin.

Were I to indulge my present feelings & give a loose to that freedom of expression which my unreserved friendship for you would prompt me to, I should say a great deal on this subject— but letters are liable to so many accidents, and the sentiments of men in office sought after by the enemy with so much avidity, and besides conveying useful knowledge (if they get into their hands) for the super structure of their plans, is often perverted to the worst of purposes, that I shall be somewhat reserved, notwithstanding this Letter goes by a private hand to Mount Vernon. I cannot refrain lamenting however in the most poignant terms, the fatal policy too prevalent in most of the states, of employing their ablest Men at home in posts of honor or profit, till the great national Interests are fixed upon a solid basis. To me it appears no unjust simile to compare the affairs of this great continent to the Mechanism of a Clock, each State representing some one or other of the smaller parts of it, which they are endeavouring to put in fine order without considering how useless & unavailing the labour, unless the great wheel, or spring which is to set the whole in motion, is also well attended to & kept in good order. I allude to no particular state nor do I mean to cast reflections upon any one of them. Nor ought I, it may be said, to do so upon their rep-

resentatives, but as it is a fact too notorious to be concealed, that
C[ongress] is rent by party—that much business of a trifling nature & personal concernment withdraws their attention from matters of great national moment at this critical period. When it is
also known that idleness and dissipation takes place of close attention and application, no man who wishes well to the liberties
of his Country & desires to see its rights established, can avoid
crying out where are our Men of abilities? why do they not come
forth to save their Country? Let this voice my dear Sir call upon
you—Jefferson & others—do not from a mistaken opinion that
we are about to set down under our own Vine and our own fig
tree let our hitherto noble struggle end in ignominy. Believe me
when I tell you there is danger of it. I have pretty good reasons
for thinking, that Administration a little while ago had resolved
to give the matter up, and negotiate a peace with us upon almost
any terms, but I shall be much mistaken if they do not now from
the present state of our Currency dissentions & other circumstances, push matters to the utmost extremity.[30]

Washington followed this letter four days later with one to James
Warren. "Our conflict is not likely to cease so soon as every good
Man would wish," he advised him.

The measure of inequity is not yet filled; and unless we can return a little more to first principles, and act a little more upon patriotic ground, I do not know when it will, or, what may be the
Issue of the contest. Speculation, Peculation, Engrossing, forestalling with all their concomitants, afford too many melancholy
proofs of the decay of public virtue; and too glaring instances of
its being the interest and desire of too many who would wish to
be thought friends, to continue the War.

Nothing I am convinced but the depreciation of our Currency
proceeding in a great measure from the foregoing Causes aided
by Stock jobbing, and party dissentions has fed the hopes of the
Enemy and kept the B[ritish] Arms in America to this day. They
do not scruple to declare this themselves, and add that, we shall
be our own conquerors. Cannot our common Country (Am.) pos-

sess virtue enough to disappoint them? Is the paltry consideration of a little dirty pelf [money] to individuals to be placed in competition with the essential rights and liberties of the present generation, and of Millions yet unborn? Shall a few designing men for their own aggrandizement, and to gratify their own avarice, overset the goodly fabric we have been rearing at the expence of so much time, blood, and treasure? and shall we at last become the victims of our own abominable lust of gain? Forbid it heaven! forbid it all and every State in the Union! by enacting and enforcing efficacious laws for checking the growth of these monstrous evils, and restoring matters in some degree to the pristine state they were in at the commencement of the War. Our cause is noble, it is the cause of Mankind! and the danger to it, is to be apprehended from ourselves. Shall we slumber and sleep then while we should be punishing those miscreants who have brot. these troubles upon us and who are aimg. to continue us in them, while we should be striving to fill our Battalions, and devising ways and means to appreciate the currency; on the credit of wch. every thing depends? I hope not. Let vigorous measures be adopted. Not to limit the price of Articles, for this I conceive is inconsistent with the very nature of things, and impracticable in itself, but to punish Speculators, forestallers, and extortioners, and above all to sink the money by heavy taxes. To promote public and private oeconomy; Encourage Manufactures &ca. Measures of this sort gone heartily into by the several States would strike at once at the root of all our evils and give the coup de grace to British hope of subjugating this Continent, either by their Arms or their Arts. The first, as I have before observed, they acknowledge is unequal to the task; the latter I am sure will be so if we are not lost to every thing that is good & virtuous.

A little time now, must unfold in some degree, the Enemys designs. Whether the state of affairs in Europe will permit them to augment their Army with more than recruits for the Regiments now on the Continent, and therewith make an active and vigorous campaign, or whether with their Florida and Canadian force they will aid and abet the Indians in ravaging our Western Frontier

while their Shipg. with detachments harrass (and if they mean to
prosecute the predatory War threatened by Administration
through their Commissioners) burn and destroy our Sea Coast; or
whether contrary to expectation, they are more disposed to negotiate than to either is more than I can determine. The latter will
depend very much upon their apprehensions of the Court of Spain,
and expectations of foreign aid and powerful alliances; at present
we seem to be in a Chaos but this cannot last long as I suppose
the ultimate determination of the British Court will be developed
at the meeting of Parliament after the Hollidays.[31]

In April, Washington complained to several correspondents about
what he perceived as the lack of virtue that had taken hold in the
country. Early in the month, he wrote to a friend in Maryland: "It is
no easy matter to develop the enemys designs—one would think it
scarcely possible that they should keep a large force in america
another campaign merely to hold possession of New York and Rhode
Island, and yet I should not be much surprized if this is the case, as
they seem to entertain great hopes from the depreciated, &
depreciating state of our currency & other causes, towards which
too many among ourselves who wish to be thought friends,
contribute not a little." It was, he wrote, "a melancholy thing" to
witness "such a decay of public virtue, and the fairest prospects
overcast & clouded by a host of infamous harpies, who to acquire a
little pelf would involve this great Continent in inextricable ruin."
He agreed with his friend's suspicion that the British had sent
"emissaries among us to promote the business of speculation in the
article of provisions, & to engross what ever is found necessary to
the existance of our Army." In Washington's view it was "true
beyond a doubt—for the enemy do not scruple to acknowledge that
their Arms are unequal to the conquest—What else can they
substitute (if they mean to persist) but their money & their arts?"[32]

And to a friend and relative in Virginia he wrote later that month:
"It is most devoutly to be wished that the several States would adopt
some vigorous measures for the purpose of giving credit to the paper
currency and punishment of speculators, forestallers and others who

are preying upon the vitals of this great Country and putting every thing to the utmost hazard—Alas what is virtue come to—what a miserable change has four years produced in the temper & dispositions of the Sons of America! It really shocks me to think of it!"[33]

Many of these same issues arose in an exchange of private letters with John Jay in April and May. On April 21, Jay penned a letter to Washington in response to a long letter from the general explaining in detail why Maj. Gen. Horatio Gates's criticisms of his generalship were unfounded. "The Delicacy, Candor & Temper diffused thro' your Letters, form a strong Contrast to the Evasions & Design observable in some others—Gratitude ought to have attached a certain Gentleman to the Friend who raised him. a spurious Ambition however, has it seems made him your Enemy." Jay then diverged into an assessment of the country and the times that reflected the views of his correspondent:

This is not uncommon. To the Dishonor of human nature, the History of Mankind has many Pages filled with similar Instances; and we have little Reason to expect that the Annals of the present, or future Times, will present us with fewer Characters of this Class. On the contrary there is Reason to expect they will multiply in the Course of this Revolution. Seasons of general Heat Tumult and Fermentation, favor the Production & Growth of some great Virtues, and of many great and little Vices. Which will predominate, is a Question which Events not yet produced, nor now to be discerned can alone determine. What Parties and Factions will arise, to what objects be directed, what Sacrifices they will require, and who will be the Victims, are Matters beyond the Sphere of human Prevision. New modes of Government not generally understood, nor in certain Instances approved—want of Moderation and Information in the People—want of Abilities & Rectitude in some of their Rulers—a wide Field open for the Operations of ambition—more raised from low Degrees to high Stations, and rendered giddy by Elevation, and the Extent of their Views—Laws dictated by the Spirit of the Times, not the Spirit of Justice and liberal Policy—Latitude in Principles as well as Commerce . . . are Circumstances that portend Evils which much Prudence vigor and Circumspection are necessary to prevent or controul. To me there appears Reason to expect a long Storm, and difficult Navigation. Calm Repose and the Sweets of undisturbed Retirement, appear more distant than a Peace with Britain.[34]

Washington answered Jay on May 10. "You give an affecting summary of the causes of the national evil we feel, and the still greater we have reason to apprehend," he wrote, "To me it appears that our affairs are in a very delicate situation; and what is not the least to be lamented is that many people think they are in a very flourishing way; and seem in a great measure insensible to the danger with which we are threatened. If Britain should be able to make a vigorous campaign in America this Summer, in the present depreciation of our money, scantiness of supplies, want of virtue and want of exertion, 'tis hard to say what may be the consequence."[35]

Later that month, after Congress had voted him extensive powers to conduct a joint campaign with French forces, Washington wrote to a delegate in Congress:

Never was there an observation founded in more truth than yours of my having a choice of difficulties. I cannot say that the resolve of Congress which you allude to has encreased them; but with propriety I may observe it has added to my embarrassment in fixing on them inasmuch as It gives me powers without the means of execution when these ought to be co-equal at least. The cries of the distressed, of the fatherless and the Widows, come to me from all quarters. The States are not behind hand in making application for assistance notwithstanding scarce any one of them, that I can find, is taking effectual measures to compleat its quota of Continental Troops, or have even power or energy enough to draw forth their Militia; each complains of neglect because it gets not what it asks; and conceives that no other suffers like itself because they are ignorant of what others experience, receiving the complaints of their own people only. I have a hard time of it and a disagreeable task. To please every body is impossible; were I to undertake it I should probably please no body. If I know myself I have no partialities. I have from the beginning, and I will to the end pursue to the best of my judgment and abilities one steady line of conduct for the good of the great whole. This will, under all circumstances administer consolation to myself however short I may fall of the expectation of others. But to leave smaller matters, I am much mistaken if the resolve of Congress hath not an eye to something far beyond our abilities; they are not, I conceive, sufficiently acquainted with the state and strength of the Army, of our resources, and how they are to be drawn out. The powers given may be beneficial, but do not let Congress deceive themselves by false expectations founded on a superficial view of the situation and circumstances of things in general and their own Troops in particular; for in a word, I give it to you as my opinion, that if the reinforcement expected by the enemy should arrive, and no effectual measures be taken to compleat our Battalions, and stop the further depreciation of our Money I do not see upon what ground we are able, or mean to continue the contest. We now stand upon the brink of a precipice from whence the smallest help plunges us headlong. At this moment, our Money does but pass; at what rate I need not add because unsatisfied demands upon the treasury affords too many unequivocal and alarming proofs to stand in need of illustration. Even at this hour every thing is in a manner, at a stand for want of this money (such as it is) and because many of the States instead of passing laws to aid the several departments of the Army have done the reverse, and hampered the transportation in such a way as to stop the Supplies wch. are indispensably necessary and for want of wch. we are embarrassd exceedingly. This is a summary of our affairs in Genl. to which I am to add that the Officers unable any longer to support themselves in the Army are resigning continually, or doing what is even worse, spreading discontent and possibly the seeds of Sedition.

You will readily perceive my good Sir that this is a confidential letter and that however willing I may be to disclose such matters and such sentiments to particular friends who are entrusted with the government of our great national concerns, I shall be extremely unwilling to have them communicated to any others, as I should feel much compunction if a single word or thought of mine was to create the smallest despair in our own people or feed the hope of the enemy who I know pursue with avidity every track which leads to a discovery of the Sentiments of Men in Office. Such (Men in Office I mean) I wish to be impressed, deeply impressed with the importance of close attention and a vigorous exertion of the means for extricating our finances from the deplorable Situation in which they now are. I never was, much less reason have I now, to be affraid of the enemys Arms; but I have no scruple in declaring to you, that I have never yet seen the time in which our affairs in my opinion were at so low an ebb as the present and witht a speedy and capitol change we shall not be able in a very short time to call out the strength and resources of the country. The hour therefore is certainly come when party differences and disputes should subside; when every Man (especially those in Office) should with one hand and one heart pull the same way and with their whole strength. Providence has done, and I am perswaded is disposed to do, a great deal for us.[36]

This perceived failure of public virtue continued to be a theme of Washington's private letters into the spring. At the end of May, Washington wrote to Lund Washington, his relation and estate manager at Mount Vernon: "Your Letter . . . which came to hand by the last Post gives a melancholy account of your prospects for a crop, and a still more melancholy one of the decay of public virtue," he lamented. "The first I submit to with the most perfect resignation and chearfulness. I look upon every dispensation of Providence as designed to answer some valuable purpose, and hope I shall always possess a sufficient degree of fortitude to bear without murmuring any stroke which may happen, either to my person or estate from that quarter. But I cannot, with any degree of patience, behold the infamous practices of speculators, monopolizers, and all that tribe of gentry which are preying upon our very vitals, and for the sake of a little dirty pelf are putting the rights and liberties of this country into the most eminent danger, and continuing a war destructive to the lives and property of the valuable part of this community, which would have ceased last fall as certainly as we now exist but for the encouragements which the enemy derived from this source, the depreciation of the money (which in a great measure is the consequence of it) and our own internal divisions."[37]

He wrote along similar lines to his friend Bryan Fairfax: "A Contest which appeared last Summer & Fall to be verging fast to a prosperous end, is now likely to be prolonged, & may rage more violently than ever—owing to a want of public virtue—Speculation, pecculation, forestalling, monopolizing, with all their concomitants, seem to have taken place of everything else, & shews in a clear point of view the depravity of human nature, in suffering a thirst for riches to absorb every other consideration, & get the better of every other duty."[38]

Finally, while in the midst of striking British outposts on the Hudson River in the summer, Washington wrote to Edmund Randolph, his friend and congressional delegate from Virginia on the difficulty of forming his operational plans without information from Congress. "I am as totally unacquainted with the political state of things, & what is going forward in the great national Council, as if I was an alien; when a competent knowledge of the temper and designs of our allies from time to time, and the frequent changes & complexion of affairs in Europe might, as they ought to do, have a considerable influence on the operations of our Army & would in many cases determine the propriety of measures which under a cloud of darkness can only be groped at." He continued:

I say this upon the presumption, that Congress, either through their own Ministers, or that of France must be acquainted, in some degree, with the Plans of G. Britn & the designs of France & Spain. . . . From what causes it proceeds I shall not undertake to say, but so the fact is, we are labouring under the effects, of two of the greatest evils that can befall a State at War, viz.—a reduced army at the begin[nin]g of a Campaign (which, more than probable, is intended for a decisive one)—and want of Money, or rather a redundancy of it; by which it is become of no value. Why timely expedients were not hit upon to guard against the first, and what measures have been, or can be, at this late hour adopted, to remove the Second, belongs to your honorable body to point out. for me, to lament the one, & feel the ill effects of the other, is all that remains.[39]

Washington thus felt that he needed to know more to plan his operations. Yet his grasp of international affairs gained from other sources was impressive, as the following letters will show. He possessed an excellent comprehension of the situation in Europe and all theaters of the war in North America. In August, in answer to a letter giving an account of Vice Admiral d'Estaing's success in the West Indies, he wrote to the French naval agent and consul at Philadelphia Jean Holker. "I feel myself honored in your polite communication. . . . The news it brings and that which I promise myself from the arms of the Count D'Estaing gives me the highest pleasure. Whilst in a victorious career of the armies of our ally, in different quarters of the world, we anticipate a reign of happiness and glory to the French nation, and tranquility and peace to America." He then surveyed the European situation: "When to the exertions, and resources of these States, we add the power and the wealth of the great house of Bourbon, it is difficult to conceive what policy could direct the court of England to a longer continuance of the war. She is already much exhausted in men, and money, and resources hence we might suppose that she cannot long resist, alone, the force which is combined against her. She may have Northern [European] assistance in view, which is the only rational solution of her obstinacy. This however may not be the case; nor will she be the first example of a people losing all eminence in the scale of nations by pursuing false measures, and vainly trusting to themselves."[40]

And he wrote later that month to Maj. Gen. John Sullivan: "European politics bear a very pleasing aspect. We have every Reason to believe that Spain has by this time taken a decided part: Great Britain having in the most explicit terms refused to accept of her mediation."[41]

As he sought to make sense of British operations in the late summer of 1779, Washington wrote Jay, giving an overview of the situation in Europe. "It really appears impossible to reconcile the conduct Britain is pursuing, to any system of prudence or policy," he explained:

Appearances are against her deriving aid from other powers; and if it is truly the case, that she has rejected the mediation of Spain, without having made allies, it will exceed all past instances of her infatuation. Notwithstanding appearances, I can hardly bring myself fully to believe that it is the case; or that there is so general a combination against the interests of Britain among the European powers, as will permit them to endanger the political ballance. I think it probable enough, that the conduct of France in the affairs of the Porte [the Ottoman Empire] and Russia will make an impression on the Empress [of Russia]; but I doubt whether it will be sufficient to counterballance the powerful motives she has to support England; and the Porte has been perhaps too much weakened in the last war with Russia to be overfond of renewing it. The Emperor [of Austria] is also the natural ally of England notwithstanding the connexions of Blood between his family and that of France; and he may prefer reasons of National policy to those of private attachment. Tis true his finances may not be in the best state, though one campaign could hardly have exhausted them, but as Holland looks up to him for her chief protection, if he should be inclined to favor England, it may give her Councils a decided biass the same way. She can easily supply what is wanting in the Article of money; and by their aid, give sinews to that confederacy. Denmark is also the natural ally of England; and though there has lately been a family bickering, her political interest may outweigh private animosity. Her marine assistance would be considerable. Portugal too, though timid and cautious at present, if she was to see connections formed by England able to give her countenance and security, would probably declare for her interests. Russia, Denmark, The Emperor, Holland, Portugal and England would form a respectable counterpoise to the opposite scale. Though all the maritime powers of Europe were interested in the independence of this Country, as it tended to diminish the overgrown power of Britain, yet they may be unwilling to see too great a preponderancy on the side of her rivals; and when the question changes itself from the seperation of America to the ruin of England as a Naval power, I should not be surprised at a proportionable change in the sentiments of some of those states which have been heretofore unconcerned Spectators or inclining to our side. I suggest these things rather as possible than probable; it is even to be expected that the decisive blow will be struck, before the interposition of the Allies England may acquire can have effect. But still as possible events, they ought to have their influence and prevent our relaxing in any measures necessary for our safety, on the supposition of a speedy peace or removal of the War from the present theatre in America.[42]

Early in the fall, as he was beginning to formulate plans for large-scale offensive action against British posts on the Hudson River, Washington wrote to Maj. Gen. Benjamin Lincoln in South Carolina: "Notwithstanding the embarrassed situation of the enemy I am far from being satisfied they will not make another and more vigorous effort to the Southward this campaign. They have very powerful motives to it," he advised.

> The *full* possession of Georgia and the acquisition of South Carolina would be a good counterpoise to their losses in the Islands: It would give credit to their cause in Europe, favour negotiations in the winter or help to gain friends for a further prosecution of the War: It would also open new sources of supplies, of which they now stand in need both on the Continent and in the West Indies, from the superiority in the English channel, which the junction of Spain must have produced and the restraint it will impose upon the exportations from England and Ireland.
> I see no better purpose to which they can apply their army in America. Inferior in naval force in the Islands, they cannot think of recovering those they have lost, or acquiring others; to garrison and preserve the remainder seems to be all they can reasonably have in view: If they make a detachment of four or five thousand men in addition to the troops already there it will in my opinion

be sufficient for this purpose. Then by evacuating Rhode Island they may spare three or four thousand more for operations in your quarter, and keep a garrison of nine or ten thousand men for the defence of New York and its dependencies, which from its particular shape and insular situation and the works they have raised and are raising, would be pretty well out of the reach of any enterprise on our part, without the co-operation of a fleet.

The possibility of an aid of this kind will indeed be an objection to the measure I am supposing, and the ideas of the enemy under their present discouragements may perhaps more naturally embrace plans of mere security than conquest. But upon the whole the probability of the latter is sufficiently great to require every precaution on our side. Southern operations appear to have been for some-time past a favourite object in the British cabinet. The weakness of the Southern states affords a strong temptation; the advantages are important and inviting, and even the desperate aspect of their affairs itself may inspire a spirit of enterprise and teach the necessity of some bold stroke to counterbalance their misfortunes and disgraces and to restore their reputation and influence.[43]

And about the same time he wrote to Maj. Gen. Lafayette, who was then in France, of news that Spain had joined the war: "The declaration of Spain in favour of France has given universal joy to every Whig, while the poor Tory droops like a withering flower under a declining Sun." He continued:

We are anxiously expecting to hear of great and important events on your side the Atlantic. At prest. the immagination is left in the wide field of conjecture. Our eyes one moment are turned to an Invasion of England, then of Ireland. Minorca, Gibralter, &ca. In a word we hope every thing, but know not what to expect or where to fix. The glorious successes of Count DEstaing in the West Indies at the sametime that it adds dominion to France and fresh lustre to her Arms is a source of *new* and unexpected misfortune to our *tender* and *generous parent* and must serve to convince her of the folly of quitting the substance in pursuit of a shadow; and as there is no experience equal to that which is bought I trust she will have a superabundance of this kind of knowledge and be convincd as I hope all the World, and every tyrant in it will that the best and only safe road to honour, glory, and true dignity, is *justice*.[44]

Toward the end of the campaign of 1779, as he waited for the arrival of a French fleet to conduct joint operations against New York City (see chapter 4), Washington wrote to his friend Edmund Pendleton. "All lesser matters, on both sides, are suspended while we are looking to the more important object," he informed Pendleton.

The consequences of all these movements are not easy to be foretold; but, another Campaign having been wasted; having had their Arms disgraced, and all their projects blasted, it may be conceiv'd that the enemy like an enraged Monster summoning his whole strength, will make some violent effort, if they should be relieved from their present apprehensions of the French fleet. If they do not detach largely for the West Indies (and I do not see how this is practicable while they remain inferior at Sea) they must from the disagreeableness of their situation feel themselves under a kind of necessity of attempting some bold, enterprizing stroke, to give, in some degree, eclat to their Arms, spirits to the Tories, and hope to the Ministry, but I am under no apprehension of a capital injury from any other source than that of the continual depreciation of our Money. This indeed is truly alarming, and of so serious a nature that every other effort is in vain unless something can be done to restore its credit. Congress, the States individually, and individuals of each state, should exert themselves to effect this great end. It is the only hope; the last resource of the enemy; and nothing but our want of public virtue can induce a continuance of the War. Let them once see, that as it is in our power, so it is our inclination and intention to overcome this difficulty, and the idea of conquest, or hope of bringing us back to a state of dependance, will vanish like the morning dew; they can no more encounter this kind of opposition than the hoar frost can withstand the rays of an all chearing Sun. The liberties and safety of this

Country depend upon it, the way is plain, the means are in our power, but it is virtue alone that can effect it, for without this, heavy taxes, frequently collected, (the only radical cure) and loans, are not to be obtained. Where this has been the policy (in Connecticut for instance) the prices of every article have fallen and the money consequently is in demand; but in other States you can scarce get a single thing for it, and yet it is with-held from the public by speculators, while every thing that can be useful to the public is engrossed by this tribe of black gentry, who work more effectually against us than the enemys Arms; and are a hundd. times more dangerous to our liberties and the great cause we are engaged in.[45]

Finally, Washington's letter to Congress on the state of the army, written at the end of the campaign of 1779, laid out the problems in manning his army that would have to be solved before the beginning of the campaign of 1780. The letter, yet another example of the American commander's detailed understanding of military affairs, summed up most of the issues he had faced in army management in 1779 and which he was to confront again in preparing for the campaign of 1780. "As the present Campaign is advancing towards a conclusion, and the Councils of the British Cabinet, so far as they have come to my knowledge, are far from recognizing our Independence and pointing to an honourable peace," he explained, "I have thought, it might not be amiss for me to lay before Congress a state of the Army . . . as it is with Congress to decide on the expediency of making it more respectable, or of fixing its amount to any particular point."

He enclosed a return that contained "a compleat view . . . of the whole strength of the forces of each [state], and of the Independent Corps." Congress could perceive by this "that our whole force *including all sorts of Troops*, non Commissioned Officers and privates, Drummers and Fifers, supposing every Man to have existed and to have been in service at that time, a point however totally inadmissible, amounted to 27,099: That of this number, comprehending 410 Invalids, 14,998 are stated as engaged for the

War: that the remainder, by the expiration of Inlistments, will be decreased by the 31st of December 2051, by the last of March 6,426, by the last of April (including the Levies) 8,181, by the last of June, 10,158: by the last of Septr. 10,709: by different periods (I believe shortly after) 12,157." But, he continued, "it will ever be found for obvious reasons, that the amount of an army on Paper, will greatly exceed its real strength." Besides other deductions "which must equally operate against the Troops of every class" there were "of necessity, very considerable and constant drafts of men from the regiments for Artificers, Armourers, Matrosses, Waggoners, the Quarter Masters Department &c., so that we cannot estimate our operating force in the Field, with any propriety or justice, by any means as high, as it may appear at first view on Paper." There was, he asserted, no "reason to expect, that these large and heavy drafts from the regiments will cease." On the contrary "it is much to be feared, from the increased and increasing difficulties in getting men, that they will be still greater."

He then proceeded to offer "with all possible deference" his "sentiments on the only mode that appears to me competent, in the present situation of things, to placing and keeping our Battalions on a respectable footing, if Congress judge the measure essential; and I trust in doing this, it will not be deemed that I have exceeded my duty. If it should my apology must be, that it proceeded from a desire to place the business of raising the Levies we may have occasion to employ in future on a more regular and certain system, than has been adopted, or at least put in practice; and from which the Public will derive the greatest benefits from their service."

In the early period of the war, he explained, "when Men might have been inlisted for the War, no Man, as my whole conduct and the uniform tenor of my letters" would show "was ever more opposed to short inlistments than I was, and while there remained a prospect of obtaining Recruits upon a permanent footing . . . I urged my sentiments in favor of it." But the prospect of maintaining the army by voluntary enlistments having faded "or at least standing on too precarious and uncertain a footing to depend on" he had laid before the committee of Congress at Valley Forge in February 1778 "a plan for an Annual draft, as the surest and most certain if not the only means left us, of maintaining the army on a proper and respectable ground." He had, he reminded Congress, once again urged the plan for annual drafts of soldiers on the committee of conference the previous January (see chapter 1) and "having reviewed it in every point of light and found it right, or at least the best that has occurred to me, I hope I shall be excused by Congress, in offering it to them and in time for carrying it into execution for the next year, if they should conceive it necessary for the States to compleat their Quotas of Troops."

He then set out the plan:

> that each State be informed by Congress annually, of the *real deficiency* of its Troops, and called upon to make it up, or such less specific number, as Congress may think proper, by a draft. That the men drafted join the Army by the 1st of January and serve 'till the first of January in the succeeding year. That from the time the drafts join the Army, the Officers of the States from which they come, be authorised and directed to use their endeavours to inlist them for the War. . . . That on or before the first of October annually, an abstract or return similar to the present one, be transmitted to Congress to enable them to make their requisitions to each State with certainty and precision. This I would propose as a general plan to be pursued, and I am persuaded it is, or one nearly similar to it will be found, the best now in our power, as it will be attended with the least expence to the Public, will place the service on the footing of order and certainty, and will be the only one that can advance the general interest to any great extent. If the plan is established, besides placing the service on the footing of more order and certainty, than it will ever otherwise be, we shall I should hope, by the exertions of the Officers, be able to increase the number of our Troops on permanent engagements for the War, especially if we should be so fortunate as to be in a condition to hold out to the drafts, that would engage, a certainty of their receiving the bounty Cloathing stipulated by the Public to be furnished their Troops, and which is so essential to the interest

of both. Cloathing is now become a superior temptation, and if
we were in circumstances to hold it out, and the drafts were sure
that they would obtain it, as they inlisted, and that it would be
regularly furnished as it became due; there are good grounds to
believe from what has been experienced, and the reports of the
Officers, that many would readily engage for the War. From these
considerations, and as it is so highly essential to the advancement
of the Public interest, both as we regard the issue of the contest,
and œconomy in men and money, I would hope, that every practicable measure will be pursued to get ample and compleat supplies of Cloathing. . . . Besides the prospect we should have of
gaining recruits for the War by having good supplies of Cloathing,
which as already observed, is become a first inducement to service.
We shall as has ever been the case, be obliged to make some issues
to the drafts, as well from principles of humanity, as to get their
service. I have been thus long on the subject of ample supplies of
Cloathing, as it is scarcely to be conceived the distresses and dis-
advantages, that flow from a deficiency. For instance, nothing can
be more injurious or discouraging, than our having only four
thousand nine hundred Blankets to distribute to the whole Army,
and so of many other Articles in but little better proportion.

Washington asserted that "The advantages of a well digested,
general Uniform system for levying recruits and bringing them to the
Army at a particular time, to serve to a fixed period are obvious."
He could then form his "plans of operation with some degree of
certainty" and determine with more exactness what he could
reasonably achieve. The periods for joining and serving that he
proposed seemed to offer the best advantage if the army was to
depend on annual drafts. "It being in January when it is proposed
that the recruits shall join, and when the Enemy cannot operate, they
will get seasoned and accustomed in some measure to a Camp life
before the Campaign opens," he explained, "and will have four or
five Months to acquire discipline and some knowledge of maneuvres,
without interruption; and their service being extended to the same
time in the succeeding Year, the Public will have all the benefits, that

can be derived from their aid, for a whole Campaign." Under the prevailing method of voluntary enlistment and very short-term drafts of militia "the Public incurs a very heavy expence, on account of the recruits . . . and scarcely receives any benefit from them. The Levies that have been raised, have come to the Army so irregularly, that the aid they were intended to give, has never been received, or at least but to a very limited and partial extent; and the time for which they were engaged, has been spent in gaining a seasoning to Camp, and discipline, when they ought to have been in the field, or they must have been sent there raw and untutored (a circumstance which may lead in some critical moment before an Enemy to most fatal consequences) and the greater part of it has been spent in Winter Quarters."[46]

As this letter shows, his chief concerns at the end of the year—as they had been all year—were men, clothing, and provisions. How, one might ask, did Washington manage to sustain himself through this myriad of difficulties? Two letters provide an answer. "It is much to be wished that Mankind in general were more disposed to accomodate difficulties than they are," he wrote to the Board of War in August. "In the circumstances of our present Warfare such a disposition is peculiarly necessary—and according to my ideas the Man who endeavours to do this—whether Civil or Military, consults well the interest of his Country. The Obstacles and difficulties which unavoidably occur are more than sufficient of themselves—and should prohibit any measures to encrease them."[47] A letter he wrote in the spring of the next year gives an even stronger indication. In May, Washington penned an epistle to Lund Washington; it is one of his most revealing letters. "New scenes are beginning to unfold themselves, which will by no means lessen my present trouble, or attention," he wrote. "You ask how I am to be rewarded for all this? There is one reward that nothing can deprive me of, & that is, the consciousness of having done My duty with the strictest rectitude, and most scrupulous exactness—and the certain knowledge, that if we should—ultimately—fail in the present contest, it is not owing to the want of exertion in me, or the application of every means that Congress and the United States, or the States individually, have put into my hands. . . . Providence—to whom we are infinitely more indebted than we are to our own wisdom—or our own exertions—has always displayed its power & goodness, when clouds and thick darkness seemed ready to overwhelm us."[48] Although he wrote these words in 1780, this answer tells us much about how Washington managed to persevere as general of the army through the trying months of 1779.

Three

Summer 1779:
Bold Strategy but Limited War

"This campaign is certainly big of events; & requires all our ex-
ertions—wisdom—fortitude—& virtue."
—Washington to his brother John Augustine
Washington, May 12, 1779

A T THE END OF APRIL, THE FRENCH MINISTER PLENIPOTENTIARY
Conrad-Alexandre Gérard, after learning that d'Estaing intended to once again bring his fleet to North America, initiated a
conference with Washington to plan for Continental army operations
with the French fleet. Gérard, accompanied by the Spanish agent to
the United States, Juan de Miralles, arrived at Washington's headquarters at Middlebrook, New Jersey, on or just before May 1 and
stayed until May 5. Regimental surgeon Dr. James Thacher recorded
the public welcome of the dignitaries on May 1: "Thirteen cannon
have just announced the arrival of M. Gérard, the French minister,
and a gentleman of distinction from Spain, by the name of Don Juan
de Mirrilliars; and preparations are making to afford these foreign
gentlemen an opportunity of reviewing our army."[1] The next day, as

Thacher indicated, Washington ordered a review of the army by Gérard and Miralles. Thacher described the event:

> The whole of our army in this quarter was paraded in martial array in a spacious field, and a stage was erected for the accommodation of the ladies and gentlemen spectators. At the signal of thirteen cannon, the great and splendid cavalcade approached in martial pomp and style. A very beautiful troop of light-horse, commanded by Major Lee, a Virginian, marched in front, then followed his excellency the commander-in-chief and his aids-de-camp, next the foreign ministers and their retinue, and the general officers of our army and their aids, closed the procession. Having arrived on the field of parade, the commander-in-chief, with the foreign ministers and general officers, passed in front of the line of the army, from right to left, in review, and received the military honors due to their rank; after which, the gentlemen dismounted and retired to the stage, and took seats with Mrs. Washington, Mrs. Greene, Mrs. Knox, and a number of other ladies, who had arrived in their carriages. The army then performed the field manoevres and evolutions, with firing of cannon and musketry. The business of the day was closed by troops deploying, and marching in front of the stage, and paying the marching salute to their excellencies. The whole performance was conducted with such marked regularity and precision, as to reflect great honor on the character of our army, and afford the commander-in-chief and the spectators the highest degree of satisfaction. On this occasion we cannot but pride ourselves on the conspicuous figure exhibited by our commander-in-chief. While mounted on his noble bay charger, his stature appears remarkable; and being a good horseman, he displays a lofty carriage, and benign dignity of demeanor, and I hope not to incur the charge of undue partiality, when I say, his appearance was incomparably more majestic and dignified than either of his illustrious visitors.[2]

But the chief purpose of Gérard's visit was to discuss potential operations of cooperation with d'Estaing. Notably, Gérard visited

Washington for these discussions *before* notifying Congress of d'Estaing's expected return. During the early part of Gérard's visit with Washington the two men held "several conferences" on plans for future operations. Washington wanted during the meetings "to convince The Minister that we are willing to make every effort in our power for striking a decisive blow." At the end of their discussions the American general prepared a letter to Gérard setting out his views on combined operations. Washington's proposals focused on New York. "As you have been pleas'd to honor me with a communication of His Excellency Count D'Estaing's intention of returning to this Continent with the Squadron under his command," he wrote Gérard, "and have desired to know my sentiments of the manner in which this event may be best improved for the interest of the common cause—and what can be done on the part of these States towards that end—I beg leave to offer the following as the definitive result, of my reflections on this subject." The American commander laid down his foremost requirement for these "joint operations." He considered "a clear superiority over the British naval force in America" the "essential basis" for "extensive combined operations." These were perhaps the most important words Washington wrote in regard to the campaign of 1779. He believed British naval supremacy had to be overturned if he was to conduct *decisive* operations. If Gérard could immediately give him "explicit assurances" that d'Estaing would "proceed with all dispatch directly from Martinique to New York" so as to arrive there before British naval reinforcements, Washington pledged that "with permission and approbation of Congress" he would "engage to relinquish all the present projects of the Campaign & collect our whole force in this quarter, with all the aid which can be drawn from the Militia of the neighbouring States, to co-operate with the Squadron of His most christian Majesty for the reduction of the enemy's Fleet & army at New York, Rhode Island and the dependencies."[3]

Washington stated that he made this commitment "from a persuasion that we should be able to collect a sufficient force to give a reasonable prospect of success to an enterprize decisive in its nature." He again requested assurances of French naval support "because without them I could not be justified in abandoning measures & engagements in which the security of these States is deeply concerned, and because a failure would be attended with the most serious mischiefs."

If the French minister could not give him such assurances he proposed an alternative plan: "That his Excellency Count D'Estaing proceed with his Squadron immediately to [Savannah] Georgia—where in conjunction with the American troops, there is every reason to believe he would with great facility capture & destroy the enemy's fleet & Army." The British could only elude capture "by a precipitate retreat to St Augustine; & even in this case, their Vessels & Stores would inevitably fall." D'Estaing should then proceed directly from Georgia to New York, where, if he arrived before British naval reinforcements "by entering the harbour expeditiously he will be sure of taking or destroying all their fleet in that Port." Washington thought that the enemy troops on Staten Island could also "be intercepted & taken" with the troops from d'Estaing's fleet landing on one part of the island and a detachment from Washington's army on another. "Successes of this kind might open a new field of action, and lead to other important events," he wrote. As an additional component of this secondary plan he proposed that on the admiral's arrival at Sandy Hook "if a few Frigates could be spared to be dispatched to Rhode Island to capture and destroy their Vessels & obstruct their retreat it would answer a very important end." He concluded his letter: "Either of these plans being pursued if attended with important successes, so as to disembarrass these States of the whole or the principal part of the enemy's force now within them, would put it in their power to co-operate with the forces of his most christian Majesty in prosecuting such offensive enterprizes against the enemy elsewhere as shall be deemed advancive of the honor and Interest of the allied powers."

But Gérard could not give him the "sufficient assurances" he sought before committing to the "great undertaking" of the first plan (which entailed giving up all the preparations for an expedition against the Iroquois), and they therefore agreed to the second plan, if and when d'Estaing returned to North America. After the meeting, the general reported to his friend Gouverneur Morris that his judgment "rather inclined" to the second plan anyway "as promising more certain success, without putting so much to the hazard." And the relief of the southern states appeared to Washington "an object of the greatest magnitude." With the accumulating evidence that a large British detachment had sailed southward, he felt "infinite anxiety" for Georgia and South Carolina. "Their internal weakness—dissaffection—the want of energy the general languor that has seized the people at large," he wrote, "makes me apprehend the most serious consequences—it would seem too, as if the enemy meant to transfer the principal weight of the war that way." Charleston, he believed, "likely will feel the next stroke—This if it succeeds will leave the enemy in full possession of Georgia by obliging us to collect our forces for the defence of South Carolina, and will consequently open new sources for men and supplies and prepare the way for a further career." Washington's greatest fear in regard to the coming of d'Estaing's fleet was that the states would fail to reinforce the army and this would result in "want of a competent land force" that would make the situation "precarious" even with the arrival of the fleet.[4]

That Gérard's visit to Washington's camp had been a success is shown by the French minister's comments afterward. His words and Washington's response show that the American commander was already mastering the diplomatic aspect of being commander in chief. "The reception that your Excellency was pleased to give me has penetrated me with gratitude," the Frenchman told Washington. "I am in pain to testify it to you, in as lively a manner, as I feel it; but another sentiment that I cannot hinder myself from testifying equally, is the admiration with which every thing I have seen has filled me more and more, for your talents and for your virtues—Envy itself and enmity are obliged to respect them and the true friends of America among whom I claim a place regard you as its glory and its hope. I have learnt better than ever to set a price on your esteem and on your kindness; and I shall think myself happy if you will permit me to count upon them."[5] The general replied: "The obligation I felt for the visit which Your Excellency did me the honor to make me could only be increased by the manner in which you are pleased to mention the reception you met with. If there was any thing that deserved to give you pleasure, it was the sentiments which accompanied the marks of respect we were happy to have an opportunity of showing you. As the Minister of a Prince we revere, you had a title to every thing we could do; but you have another title, not less precious to your sensibility—all the true friends of America esteem it an honor to rank you among their number, and acknowlege the distinguished instances you have given of your zealous concern for its interests."[6]

After his conference with Washington, Gérard advised Congress of d'Estaing's intention to return to the North American coast. On May 9, he sent a letter to Congress. He explained that at their request he had some time ago written to the admiral to request that he come to the aid of Georgia. Gérard had proposed a plan for joint operations in Georgia, but Congress had gone silent on the project. But "the answer of that vice admiral having reached me, I do not think, Sir, that the interest of the alliance and of these states will permit me to conduct myself according to the presumed negative resolution of Congress," he declared. He accompanied his letter with an "annexed memoire" setting out the French position and expectations. In it, he advised Congress that d'Estaing had answered him "that the superiority of the enemy had not hitherto permitted him to leave those shores [the West Indies]. But that in consequence of his majesty's intentions, which are to grant to the united states his allies all the succour compatible with the security of his own possessions and the general position of affairs, he proposes immediately to come to the southern coast of the states and labour for the deliverance of Georgia and the preservation of South Carolina." From there "his majesty's squadron" would sail "to the mouth of the Delaware, and their ulterior operations will depend upon the concert, which shall be taken between the Congress and the commander of his majesty's forces and shall be calculated for the greatest advantage of the united states."

Gérard, in a strong hint that France expected the United States to conduct important and successful joint operations with d'Estaing's fleet, advised Congress that he desired that body would "inform him from time to time of what shall have been done in the premisses particularly as the minister must answer personally for measures the ill success of which would expose to the greatest misfortunes a force which the king has destined for the direct and immediate succour of the united states."[7]

With this strong notice that the French expected joint operations, Congress acted swiftly. It granted Washington sweeping powers over strategy and operations. On May 10, it passed an act declaring that Washington should "consider himself at liberty so to direct the military operations of these states as shall appear to him most expedient."[8] On the same day, John Jay, president of Congress, sent Washington a copy of the act and informed him that "Congress confide fully in your Excellency's Prudence and Abilities." He assured Washington that they wished him to place reliance on his own judgment and that he need only communicate his plans as he judged necessary or expedient.[9]

Assured of Washington's grasp of strategy after his meetings with the committee of conference and his meeting with Gérard, and even more confident in Washington's judgment to plan and execute operations with the French, Congress gave him wide discretion. In stark contrast with attitudes held as recently as the winter of 1778, that body thus vested Washington with complete power to plan and conduct combined operations with the French. There were no more rivals. He now had complete authority over military operations on the continent. This great confidence in his generalship reflected his leadership at the Battle of Monmouth, his performance in the campaign of 1778—the first with the French—and the strategic planning and administrative abilities the commander in chief had demonstrated in his extended discussions with Congress the previous winter.[10] Such unyielding trust and confidence in him by Congress firmed up Washington's position as commander in chief and certainly must have increased his confidence in preparing for joint operations with the French.

Despite these broad powers, the American commander had to keep his strategic goals very limited. With Gérard having committed to only a limited, contingent campaign at New York and no certain guarantee that d'Estaing would come to cooperate with him, Washington moved to carry out the plan of campaign he had formulated earlier in the year with Congress: launching an expedition against the Iroquois in western New York to relieve the frontiers, while keeping the main army "intirely on the defensive" and focusing on recruiting its regiments to full strength.

Despite his limited means and myriad difficulties, Washington wanted to push the war as vigorously as possible. His letter to his brother John Augustine Washington provides the best record of his outlook at this time: "I [give] it to you clearly as my opinion, that the enemy will strain every nerve to push the War with vigor this Campaign—By accts from England . . . it appears evident that Seven Regiments besides two of the new raised scotch Corps[,] recruits for the Guards, & for other Regiments now in america were on the point of embarking." He believed that the British would garrison New York and Rhode Island strongly, and "push their successes to the Southward vigorously." Because of American financial, supply, and recruiting difficulties, the British ministry, he thought, would certainly "try the event of another campaign; in which they will exert all their cunning & the force of the Kingdom." Urging his brother to become a member of the state legislature, Washington concluded: "This is no time for slumbering & sleeping; nor to dispute upon trifles, when our Battalions are to fill—supplies to provide. & ruined finances to recover & at a crisis when G. Britain is ready to pour forth her utmost vengeance. . . . This campaign is certainly big of events; & requires all our exertions—wisdom—fortitude—& virtue."[11]

"My Ideas of contending with the Indians have been uniformly the same—and I am clear in opinion—that the most oeconomical . . . as well as the most effectual mode of opposing them—where they can make incursions upon us—is to carry the war into their own Country." Washington wrote this to Congressman James Duane in January. This was the philosophy that drove his conception of what he called "the Western Expedition."[12]

The expedition against the Iroquois, designed to relieve the pressure on the New York and Pennsylvania frontiers, was the centerpiece of Washington's design for the campaign of 1779, and he dedicated much time and effort to its planning. Washington planned the expedition in detail over the course of the winter and spring and spent much of the summer arranging arms, supplies, and militia support for the expedition. To aid his planning, he consulted local governors and his officers assigned to duty in the west. He also sought information and advice from New Yorker and former Continental general Philip Schuyler.[13] He chose Maj. Gen. John Sullivan to command the expedition.[14] Washington's goal was the utter destruction of the Iroquois' ability to wage war.

His instruction to Sullivan was to establish a central post "in the center of the Indian Country" from where "parties should be detached to lay waste all the settlements around with instructions to do it in the most effectual manner, that the country may not be merely overrun but destroyed." The American commander suggested several "general rules" to govern Sullivan's operations: "to make rather than receive attacks, attended with as much impetuosity, shouting and noise as possible, and to make the troops act in as loose and dispersed a way as is consistent with a proper degree of government concert and mutual support—It should be previously impressed upon the minds of the men wherever they have an opportunity, to rush on with the war [w]hoop and fixed bayonet—Nothing will disconcert and terrify the Indians more than this." Knowing the Iroquois to be a formidable enemy, Washington urged on Sullivan "the necessity of using every method in your power, to gain intelligence of the enemy's strength motions and designs" and recommended an "extraordinary degree of vigilance and caution . . . to guard against surprises from an adversary so secret desultory & rapid as the Indians." Finally, he made the overarching goal clear: "But you will not by any means listen to any overture of peace before the total ruin of their settlements is effected."[15] Washington assigned four brigades totaling over five thousand officers and men to the expeditionary army. But he kept the main army near the Hudson River to defend West Point and the important posts on that river. A British attack up the Hudson in June did not deter Washington from launching the expedition.

After much delay assembling troops, equipment, and gathering supplies at Wyoming, Pennsylvania, Sullivan carried out the offen-

Lake Ontario

Onondaga Lake

Skaneateles Lake

Owasco Lake

Cayuga Lake

Seneca Lake

Genesee Castle
(Chenussio)
Sept. 14

Canandaigua

Sept. 9   Canandesaga

Canandaigua Lake

Keuka Lake

Sept. 15

Kendaia

Catherine's Town
(Shechquago)   Sept. 23

Genesee River

Chemung River

Newton
Aug. 29

Chemung

Tioga
Aug. 11
(ret. Sept. 30)

NEW YORK

PENNSYLVANIA

N

Wyon
July

West Branch of the Susquehanna River

Susquehanna River

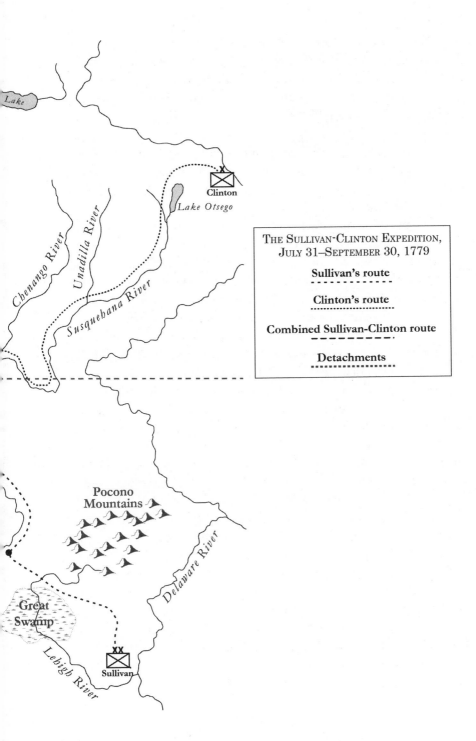

THE SULLIVAN-CLINTON EXPEDITION,
JULY 31–SEPTEMBER 30, 1779

Sullivan's route

Clinton's route

Combined Sullivan-Clinton route

Detachments

sive between August 26 and September 28. The expeditionary army defeated a combined British, Loyalist, and Indian force at the Battle of Newtown, New York, on August 29 and destroyed numerous Iroquois villages in their march up the Susquehanna River and through the Finger Lakes region to the Genesee River.[16] The goal of destruction was fulfilled. Although the war-making power of the Iroquois was not broken, because they could be supplied from British resources at Niagara, the threat to the western frontier was abated for the remainder of the campaigning season, allowing Washington to focus on the New York City area.

While planning the attack on the Iroquois, Washington was exercising the diplomatic aspect of his role as commander in chief with the neutral Delaware Indians. A delegation of Delaware had arrived in Philadelphia on May 4 for meetings with Congress and traveled to Washington's headquarters at Middlebrook, New Jersey, to see the general. He met with the chiefs and councilors on the afternoon on May 12. The Indians presented an address, which they also intended to deliver to Congress, in which they asserted their nation's status as "a free & independent People" and reaffirmed their policy of "a strict neutrality" in the war. They declared their nation's "firm Resolution to continue an inviolate Friendship with the United States of America to the End of Time." They repudiated a treaty signed at Fort Pitt in September 1778 by Brig. Gen. Lachlan McIntosh and some Delaware chiefs to provide guides and supplies for McIntosh's projected expedition against Detroit. The treaty had divided and unsettled the nation and the delegation claimed that McIntosh had misled the chiefs and that the agreement "contained Declarations & Engagements they never intended to make or enter into." They asked that Congress fulfill its promise, made in successive treaties, to supply the Delawares with clothing and other goods "absolutely necessary for the Subsistence of their Women & Children." They asked Washington to "give such Orders as will prevent any further Infringement of the Friendship & Alliance subsisting between the said Delaware Nation & the United States of America" agreeable to treaty. They hoped that the answer of Congress and Washington "may cement & make an everlasting Union between their respective Nations."[17]

During his meeting with the delegation, Washington delivered a formal reply. Addressing his answer to "the Chief Men, Deputies from the Delaware Nation," Washington told the Indians that he was happy to see them in his camp, and he wrote, "I am glad the long Journey you have made, has done you no harm; and that you are in good health. I am glad also you left All our friends of the Delaware Nation well." The American general recognized that the matters covered in the delegation's paper were "weighty things," and he continued, "I have considered them well." Noting that the Delaware nation had shown their "good will" to the United States, he rejoiced "in the new assurances you give of their friendship." Declaring "I am a Warrior," he told the chiefs: "My words are few and plain; but I will make good what I say. 'Tis my business to destroy all the Enemies of these States and to protect their friends. You have seen how we have withstood the English for four years. . . . We have till lately fought the English all alone. Now the Great King of France is become our Good Brother and Ally. He has taken up the Hatchet with us, and we have sworn never to bury it, till we have punished the English and made them sorry for All the wicked things they had in their Hearts to do against these States." He hoped that his words would "sink deep" into their hearts. He then stated his view of Indian relations: "We love our Friends—and will be faithful to them—as long as they will be faithful to us. We are sure our Good brothers the Delawares will always be so. But we have sworn to take vengeance on our Enemies—and on false friends." He explained that he was sorry to hear that the Delawares had suffered for lack of necessary supplies, and he referred them to Congress for action on that point. "I hope you will receive satisfaction from them." As to the attacks they had reported, he assured the delegation "I will do every thing in my power to prevent your receiving any further injuries and will give the strictest orders for this purpose. I will severely punish any that shall break them." He ended his reply on a diplomatic note: "When you have seen all you want to see, I will then wish you a good Journey to Philadelphia. I hope you may find there every thing your hearts can wish, that when you return home you may be able to tell your Nation good things of us—And I pray god he may make your

Nation wise and Strong, that they may always see their own true interest and have courage to walk in the right path; and that they never may be deceived by lies to do any thing against the people of these States, who are their Brothers and ought always to be one people with them."[18] Seeking to impress the delegation with the strength and discipline of his army, Washington ordered several of the brigades to parade, and he passed in front of the line and reviewed the troops with the Indian chiefs.[19]

At the conclusion of the delegation's visit, Washington wrote John Jay, president of Congress, with a summary of his meeting with the Delaware chiefs: "They presented me with a long memorial on various points, which they intend to present also to Congress. I was a little at a loss what answer to give and could have wished they had made their first application there. But as an answer could not be avoided—I thought it safest to couch it in general but friendly terms and refer them to Congress for a more particular one. Though there is reason to believe, they have not adhered very scrupulously to their pretended friendship—it appeared to me to be our present policy at least to conciliate; and in this spirit my answer was conceived."[20]

To ensure the safe return of the delegation, Washington ordered Col. Daniel Brodhead at Fort Pitt to meet them along their return route with an escort of troops. And, fulfilling his promise to punish those attacking Delaware, he directed Brodhead to court-martial a Virginia soldier accused of murdering a young Delaware man and make sure some Delaware were present at his punishment.[21] The Delaware Indians fragmented in the latter years of the war. Some remained neutral, but some warriors joined the British. A detachment of Delaware warriors served with the Continental army until the end of the war.[22]

The Sullivan expedition fulfilled the strategy agreed between Washington and Congress in the winter. But Washington had to keep his main army on the defensive watching the British army in the New York City area. British moves in the summer, though, led Washington to look for additional opportunities to strike counter-blows against his more mobile enemy.

Having withdrawn from Philadelphia the previous summer to husband forces for the expansion to new theaters with the entry of France into the war, the British developed a new strategy for the campaign of 1779. Historian Piers Mackesy, in his classic history of the war, succinctly set out the new British strategy and the reasons behind it:

> In the first two campaigns of the war, the aim had been to break the rebellion by crushing its army and overrunning its political centres. The result had been that while the American army had survived, the British had failed to consolidate their territorial gains. . . . The military master-plan having failed, it was necessary to attempt a more systematic consolidation: to break away from the search for an enemy centre of gravity, to recognize the atomised political and social structure of the colonies, and to subordinate the military to the political aspect of the problem. . . . If this reasoning was sound, the piecemeal reduction of separate colonies might achieve what the search for a single point of effort had failed to do. If the regular army could not destroy Washington, its role must be to drive him out and fend him off, while internal order in the recovered colonies was established by a loyalist militia.[23]

On January 23, 1779, Lord George Germain, the British secretary of state for America, sent Clinton the outline of the campaign plan for 1779. Germain, speaking for the ministry of a plan approved by the king, urged Clinton "to bring Mr. Washington to a general and decisive action at the opening of the campaign." If Clinton could not achieve that goal, he was to force Washington "to seek for safety in the Highlands of New York or the Jersies" which the ministry hoped would induce the inhabitants of those states to return to allegiance to the crown. Clinton was also to form two corps of four thousand men each and, assisted by the navy, employ them on the seacoasts of the states—one corps against New England, the other against the states on Chesapeake Bay. The expeditions were to seize and destroy shipping and stores and to stop the fitting out of privateers, thus blocking foreign commerce of the states. Meanwhile Indians and provincial forces on the frontiers were to make "a considerable diversion" by "alarming and harassing the frontiers and making incursions into the settlements." Clinton was authorized to make alterations in the plan if necessary to fit actual conditions. Germain promised Clinton 6,600 reinforcements to carry out this strategy. He informed Clinton that the reinforcement would be sent out "early in the spring."[24]

Raids on the American coast were a key part of the strategy for 1779. Lord Amherst, the chief commander of the British army in England and Clinton's superior, favored systematic coastal raiding, a policy he had advocated since 1777. General James Robertson also advocated raiding expeditions. Germain, despite the hatred he must have known raiding would instill in the victims, made raiding expeditions part of the plan because it could hinder privateering, damage the states' economies, and pin down rebel militias.[25] The orders from Germain reached Clinton in New York on April 24.[26] Clinton put the strategy into execution in the summer. He had already devised a plan for raids, based on suggestions from Germain the previous fall.[27]

Clinton believed that Washington's main army in the camp at Middlebrook, about eight thousand strong, with militia ready to support it, was too strong to attack without reinforcements. "My plan," Clinton later wrote, "was consequently to endeavor by indirect maneuvers to draw him forward before the new levies from the different states should have time to join him, and then move against him while in motion, or force him into a general and decisive action by placing myself between him and his magazines at Trenton. But, as this latter might have led me too far from New York and my other posts, all that I could do for the present was to put matters in forwardness against the arrival of the expected succors."[28]

While Washington remained encamped at Middlebrook with the main army waiting to see what move Clinton would make, that general, while waiting for reinforcements from Great Britain, decided to launch a "desultory expedition" to the Chesapeake. The expedition was part of a larger plan:

when the attention of the enemy should by these operations be turned to the southward, it was planned that the armament should suddenly return and join in a move I proposed making up the North River against the rebel forts that covered King's Ferry. And, should the English and West Indies reinforcements join me at that critical moment . . . it was my intention to extend my views even to attacking the works at West Point. An action with Mr. Washington's army was likewise comprised within the operations I proposed.

If Clinton could tempt Washington into an action for the defense or recovery of the King's Ferry forts, the British general rightly believed he would have a great tactical advantage: the American commander would be pinned in between the mountains and the river, but Clinton, with the Royal Navy in control of the river, could withdraw without risk.[29] Thus, even an operation to strike Virginia had as its goal the forts on the Hudson and Washington's main army.

At the beginning of May, Clinton set in motion the raiding expedition to the Chesapeake. His goals were to delay the dispatch of the Virginia troops being raised to reinforce Washington's army by spreading alarm, destroy the supply magazines and naval stores collected there, and destroy the warships building or fitting out there.[30] Clinton placed Maj. Gen. Edward Mathew in command of the land force and Commodore George Collier, then commanding the North American station, in command of the naval force. In support of his overall plan, Clinton ordered Collier and Mathew to return by June 1. Collier's small naval squadron included one sixty-four-gun ship of the line, one forty-four-gun frigate, three sloops of war, one galley, several privateers, and twenty-two transports. Mathew's force composed the grenadier and light infantry companies of the British Guards, the British 42nd Infantry Regiment, the Loyalist Volunteers of Ireland Regiment, and the Hessian Prince Charles Regiment, in total about two thousand troops. The troops embarked at New York on May 1.

The expedition caught Virginia unprepared to meet such a raid. The squadron and transports sailed from Sandy Hook on May 5 and the raiders landed near Portsmouth on May 10. Mathew's troops captured the fort and town the same day. Defenders burned a Continental warship in the port and the British troops destroyed two warships being constructed in the shipyard and two French merchant ships. The Patriots could offer little resistance. Brig. Gen. Charles Scott, the senior Continental officer in the state, kept Washington abreast of the raid, but because of the distance, Washington could do nothing to aid Virginia. The state, Scott reported, was "almost totally unprepared" to oppose the raid. The Virginia militia evacuated the fort at Portsmouth and all its military stores were lost. In hopes of providing a better defense, Scott ordered down the new Continental levies he had been raising in Fredericksburg and Alexandria. Encountering no opposition, a detachment of Mathew's corps marched to Suffolk, burned the town, and destroyed or captured about one third of the five thousand barrels of salted pork stored there. But militia assembled by two colonels sent down by Scott covered the remaining stores. Once again meeting no resistance, the British returned to Portsmouth, burned the barracks there, destroyed the fort, freed slaves, and took off a large quantity of tobacco and the military stores.

For the next seven days, Mathew's troops raided storehouses and magazines and attacked various outposts in the Norfolk-Portsmouth area. But slowly the Virginia militia began to assemble. When on the twenty-fifth a force appeared off Hampton, and made some attempts to land, the sight of militia under arms caused them to go off. The raiders inflicted heavy damage on shipping, destroying four other ships besides those in Portsmouth and captured one. Including smaller vessels, Collier claimed to have destroyed a total of 130 ships and vessels on the raid. They also captured valuable naval stores in the Portsmouth shipyard. With Clinton's June 1 return date approaching, Mathew loaded the captured stores on Collier's ships and on May 24 re-embarked his troops. The expedition forces were back in New York on May 29.[31]

Clinton was well satisfied with the raid on the Chesapeake. "Every object" of the expedition, he later wrote, "was fully attained even beyond my most sanguine expectations. For, besides the universal terror and alarm which this armament spread on its arrival through every part of the country bordering on that great expanse of water, the loss which the enemy sustained from its operations was prodigious."[32]

Of course, Washington took a different view of the raid. He expressed his view in a private letter to his brother John Augustine Washington: "I am very sorry to hear that the plunder taken from Virginia by the detachment commanded by Genl Matthews was so immense; it is some consolation and indeed pleasure to hear that a large part of it belonged to speculators. I am equally concerned to hear that they have done this without opposition, Their own papers boast of the destruction and consequent injury to us, without the loss of a single man. This does not reflect much honor upon the spirit of my Countrymen. They might, they ought to have bestowed a few guns if no more, upon the party that moved to Suffolk. Riches so easily and cheaply purchased will be a powerfull inducement to another visit. Wealth even among the boasting sons of Britain has charms more powerful than honor and glory acquired by hard knocks."[33] This type of war frustrated Washington. Responding to Jay's transmission of letters from Virginia governor Patrick Henry on the raid, Washington wrote: "The predatory war which the enemy now seem resolved to carry on will be very distressing—little aid can be afforded from the army in its present situation and the militia appear to be too ill provided with arms to defend themselves."[34] More soon followed.

With the return of Mathew and Collier, Clinton immediately executed the second part of his plan—the attack on the forts guarding the strategically vital King's Ferry crossing of the Hudson River. He attacked in hopes that his promised reinforcements would arrive in time to exploit any advantages he might gain.

Even before Collier and Mathew returned, Washington became aware of Clinton's preparations, and he took defensive measures. He alerted Maj. Gen. Alexander McDougall, the commander at West Point, and directed Maj. Gen. Israel Putnam, commanding on the west side of the Hudson, to be ready to send Brig. Gen. Samuel Holden Parsons' brigade to "March without a moments loss of time" to aid McDougall if the British attacked West Point.[35] For his expedition up the Hudson, Clinton assembled an overwhelmingly large attack force composed of the light infantry, the British and Hessian grenadiers, the 17th, 63rd, 33rd, and 64th Regiments of Foot, three hundred jaegers, and three provincial regiments. Combined with Mathew's corps, the total came to over six thousand troops.

Clinton's attack was swift. He landed his force on May 31 near King's Ferry on both sides of the river. Maj. Gen. James Pattison, with the 17th, 63rd, and 64th Foot and a hundred jaegers, commanded the western force, landing three miles below Stony Point. The fort at that post was unfinished. On the approach of Pattison's regiments, the Continental garrison burned the blockhouse and evacuated the fort. The fort at Stony Point, being on higher elevation, commanded the fort at Verplanck Point across the river. In the course of the night, the British brought up artillery to bombard Verplanck Point. The British also began completing and strengthening the fort at Stony Point. Maj. Gen. John Vaughan, commanding the eastern force, landed eight miles below Fort Lafayette at Verplanck Point. Vaughan's force, composed of the grenadiers and the light infantry, the remaining jaegers, and the provincial regiments, marched up to Fort Lafayette and surrounded it. That fort's garrison consisted of only a captain and seventy men. On June 1, the British began a bombardment of Verplanck Point from the battery at Stony Point. Vaughan by that time had completely invested Verplanck Point. Bombarded by artillery at Stony Point and the galleys in the river and surrounded by Vaughan's corps, the garrison of Verplanck Point capitulated late on the afternoon of June 1. On June 3, Clinton, with the force on the east side of the river, advanced to Peekskill on a reconnaissance and stopped just short of the Continental Village, a supply post and camp of the Continental army established in 1776, three miles north of Peekskill. The British forces then settled down to fortify Stony Point.[36]

Learning of Clinton's advance, Washington reacted rapidly. He marched from Middlebrook with the Pennsylvania, Virginia, and Maryland divisions to support McDougall, but his move was slowed by difficulty in procuring wagons, horses, and forage.[37] To the commander of the Virginia division he wrote, "I request you will exert yourself to get the division under yr command in instant readiness to march at an hours warning. It will point towards The North River. I have received some recent intelligence which makes it necessary we should be in motion."[38] Col. William Malcom, commanding the New York militia on the west side of the river, also moved to defend West Point.[39] Washington arrived too late to prevent British occupation of the posts, but the move to New York prevented any British push farther north to attack West Point.

Clinton had expected to provoke a major action with the attack: "This pass [ferry] was of such great importance to the enemy that I fully expected Mr. Washington would have risked an action for its recovery." With that in mind, the British general left much of his attack force at King's Ferry and, with the remainder of his force, took up a central position at Philipsburg (Yonkers) within a day's march (or sail) of King's Ferry and New York to await the arrival of his expected reinforcements.[40]

But the American general did not grant his wish. Washington did not want to be drawn into a battle against Clinton's full army for the recovery of King's Ferry. Forts can only be taken by surprise or siege and the American commander could not undertake a siege with Clinton's army threatening the far more important West Point and with the British having mobility on the river to get behind Washington's army. But, on the other hand, Clinton felt he did not have sufficient force to attack West Point, the one post Washington would fight to retain.

Thus, Clinton had not been able to bring his plan to fruition. His campaign plan, he later claimed, had been hamstrung by the failure of the promised reinforcements to arrive. "Had the promised reinforcements arrived in any *reasonable* time, my opening the campaign thus early had given me every advantage over the enemy I could wish." He also thought his strike up the Hudson had prevented any possibility of an American attack on Canada. He believed he now held positions that would allow him either to strike from the river with his troops to cut Washington's communications, or, alternatively, to seize Washington's former camp at Middlebrook cutting off his supplies from New Jersey and simultaneously threatening Sullivan's base at Easton, Pennsylvania. Such moves, he believed, would bring Washington to fight a general action. Clinton also held out the option of attacking West Point. But he could, he felt, only be strong enough to implement these plans if he received his six thousand reinforcements. Without them he could only secure his posts at New York and on the Hudson and remain in New York "watching the course of events."[41] But his offensive had nevertheless had an impact. By drawing Washington out of New Jersey where the Continental army was close to its supplies, Clinton's attack on the Hudson had forced the American general to take a position on the Hudson where supplying his army was far more difficult.

Washington very quickly identified Clinton's strategy: "Their movements and conduct are very perplexing—and leave it difficult to determine what are their real Objects," he wrote to Congress. "However, as the posts in the Highland's are of infinite consequence and the points, in which we can be most essentially injured, I shall take every measure in my power to provide for their security—and accordingly shall make such a disposition of the Army as shall best promise to answer the end. If they should not operate against those posts—it would seem that one part of their expedition and a principal one, is to cut off the communication by the way of King's ferry, by establishing Garrisons."[42] Five days later Washington advised Congress why Clinton's move was so damaging: "They continue fortifying & no doubt mean to keep possession of those posts—The natural strength of the ground with very little help of art will make them inaccessible to us in our present circumstances—The advantages of holding them will be important to the enemy—the inconveniences to us great. It is a step to further operations against the forts—Our communication by Kings ferry, far the easiest, is at an end—The extent and difficulty of land transportation considerably increased—a new resort and sanctuary afforded to the disaffected in these parts of the country—and a new door opened to draw supplies distress and corrupt the inhabitants."[43]

After the attack, Washington's strategic outlook shifted to the defense of West Point and watching the British. He believed, rightly, that Clinton had designs on West Point, but he was not totally sure of Clinton's future moves. Near the end of June he wrote to a friend: "Their first movement from New York pointed so directly to our Posts in the Highlands that I repaired as quick as possible to their relief, but whether they found the garrisons in a better condition to receive them than they expected—or whether they only meant to possess themselves of the best, indeed (for us) only passage of the River below the highlands, thereby making the communication betwn the East & West side more circuitous & difficult, I shall not undertake to say, but it was certainly one of the wisest measures they have yet pursued to stop at, & fortify this place."[44] "The apparent design however of this movement was an attack upon our posts in the highlands," he informed his brother John Augustine. "But after dispossessing us of a small post at Kings Ferry . . . they set themselves down on both sides and began to fortify with astonishing industry. The spots they have chosen are to all intents and purposes, Islands— strong by nature and almost inaccessible by land, but open and exposed to their shipping, which ever has, and ever will give us immense trouble till there can be a counterbalance. At present it is a source of much mischief & great perplexity to us as there is no counteracting them." He was unsure whether his march into New York or the strength of the West Point garrison "prevented the prosecution of their plan, or whether by taking possession of the best crossing place below the mountains, they meant to render the communication between the East and West side of the river more circuitous and difficult, and consequently our cover of the Country more intricate, dangerous, and ineffectual . . . is more than I can decide with any degree of certainty; though it is beyond a doubt that while the Enemy retain their present position I must hold mine."[45]

Washington thus deployed his army around West Point and concentrated on bolstering its defenses against the expected arrival of British reinforcements. "I am now putting our fortifications in the highlands (which are the security of the River, & the communication between the Eastern & Southern States) in the best posture of defence I can till the enemy by some further demonstration announce their Plan of operations for the Campaign," he explained to a friend.[46] He considered defense of the fortress "a great and primary object."[47] Showing the emphasis Washington placed on the defense of West Point, he issued contingency orders to his generals for the defense of the post, specifying assignments for the garrison and each of the army's three divisions.[48] He directed McDougall to move his headquarters to West Point and take command of the forts.[49] On June 21, Washington shifted his headquarters to New Windsor, about five miles north of West Point. "Where," he explained to Congress, "I am more contiguous to the forts and best situated to attend to the different parts of the army."[50] Starting in July, the American commander moved the fortification of West Point into high gear, constructing eight new redoubts and batteries to guard the main forts (Fort Putnam and Fort Arnold) and increasing the number of cannon in the fortifications.[51] Washington himself surveyed the works and directed that an additional redoubt be added at a critical location on a hill above Fort Putnam, one of the fortress's main bastions.[52] He deployed his army on both sides of the river in terrain that favored defense—New York's Hudson Highlands. Maj. Gen. Israel Putnam commanded the wing stationed west of the Hudson, with six brigades totaling over 5,200 Continentals (organized into the three divisions of Major Generals Johann Kalb, Arthur St. Clair, and William Alexander, Lord Stirling). Brig. Gen. Anthony Wayne's corps of light infantry was also on this side of the Hudson at old Fort Montgomery (Wayne operated directly under Washington's orders). Maj. Gen. William Heath commanded the wing of the army on the east side of the Hudson, with four brigades of over 3,800 Continentals; two of these formed Maj. Gen. Robert Howe's forward division, which also included two regiments of dragoons and a partisan corps. Three additional brigades totaling 2,200 men formed the garrison of West Point. But Washington also began planning for a limited offensive to retake the King's Ferry forts.[53]

In early July, Clinton struck again, this time on the Connecticut coast. He intended to draw Washington out of the Highlands. Washington having deployed the majority of his forces on the west side of the Hudson to protect West Point, Clinton perceived an opening: "And in the meantime, as the enemy had but few troops below the Highlands on the east side of the river and those chiefly cavalry, I thought it very probable that, if I should send a corps into Connecticut, the cries of that province might stir him from his position and, by the suddenness of his passage across the North River, possibly afford an opening either of attacking some part of his army."[54]

Clinton embarked a corps of about 2,600 men under the command of Maj. Gen. William Tryon, directing him to descend on New Haven, Fairfield, Stratford, and Milford "for the purpose of destroying public stores, privateers, etc., and doing the enemy every other injury he could consistent with humanity."[55] Tryon, with Brig. Gen. Garth, commanded a battalion of guards, three British regiments, a detachment of jaegers, a Hessian regiment, and the (Loyalist) King's American Regiment. The expedition left New York on July 3. Tryon's raiders descended on New Haven on July 5, destroying public stores, ordnance, and shipping. Landings at Fairfield (on July 8) and Norwalk (on July 11) followed, with magazines, stores, and vessels again destroyed. Clinton admitted in his memoirs that Tryon's men put the latter two towns to the torch in revenge for inhabitants firing on them from their houses. Apparently in retaliation for the opposition offered by the militia to his march to the town, during which his troops were "under a continual fire," General Garth intended to start a "conflagration" in New Haven, "which he thought it merited." But he relented when no shots were fired the next day at his retreating troops; he burned "only the public stores, some vessels and ordnance," and an armed privateer ship. In Fairfield, two churches were burned. Unlike the raid on Virginia, Tryon found that militia quickly assembled to oppose his force. The Connecticut militiamen soon began to inflict losses on Tryon's regiments. "The rebels in arms at New Haven were considerable," Tryon advised Clinton, "more numerous at Fairfield, and still more so at Norwalk."[56] Brig. Gen. Samuel Holden Parsons soon joined the militia opposing the raid with 250 Continentals.

Washington responded to the raid, but not in the force Clinton had hoped. As soon as he learned of the embarkation and suspecting that the Connecticut coast might be its objective, Washington ordered Brig. Gen. John Glover with his brigade, already in Connecticut, to form a junction with the militia and "take measures with them for counteracting & repelling their attempts."[57] Washington also directed General Heath, commanding on the east side of the Hudson, to march toward Connecticut with the two brigades to give "aid and countenance" to the militia "to repress" the British "depredations."[58] Washington could do little more and wrote with anguish to officials in Norwalk: "The depredations and ravages of the Enemy upon your coast, give me great concern and I sincerely regret that the means of protection in my power, are not equal to my wishes. You may be assured that whatever I can do to afford relief shall be done."[59]

Parsons reported to Washington on July 9 that Tryon's men plundered New Haven, "destroyd Fairfield, almost every House: the Abuses of Women, Children & Old Men are unparaleld."[60] Washington, again showing his disgust with this type of warfare, in a report to Congress noted that "plundering" and "burning" now appeared "to form a considerable part of their present system of War."[61] The destruction wrought in the raid was no accident. Tryon admitted in his report to Clinton that his purpose was to awaken "a general terror and despondency" in the people of Connecticut and counteract "a presumptuous confidence in our forbearance."[62] Washington wanted to strike back on England: "If it is practicable," he urged Congress, "it seems to me, high time to retaliate by destroying some of their Towns."[63]

Despite his anger over the attack on Connecticut, Washington did not take the bait of Tryon's raid. He kept his focus on the Hudson, despite his feeling for the inhabitants of Connecticut. The Connecticut militia was assembling to oppose Tryon's raiders. Clinton put a stop to Tryon's raid, a decision he attributed to Washington's determination "not to stir from his position."[64] Washington recalled Heath after learning that Tryon had left Connecticut.[65]

The Hudson River crossing at King's Ferry, with its forts at Stony Point on the west bank and Verplanck Point on the east bank, held great strategic value. It became the focus of Washington's operations.

Always aggressive, Washington had begun planning for assaults against the posts even before the raids on Connecticut. Upon General Wayne's appointment to command the army's elite brigade of light infantry, Washington gave him his "general instructions" for Wayne's conduct as commander of the light infantry. "The importance of the two posts of Verplanks & Stoney points to the enemy is too obvious to need explanation. We ought if possible to disposses them." He directed Wayne to gain a knowledge of all aspects of the posts, their garrisons, and the surrounding territory. "It is a matter I have much at heart to make some attempt upon these posts."[66] But the British raids on the Connecticut coast increased the urgency of an attempt to retake King's Ferry. Washington felt it essential that the army respond to the raids. As he wrote to Wayne on July 9: "While the enemy are making excursions to distress the country it has a very disagreeable aspect to remain in a state of inactivity on our part—the reputation of the army and the good of the service seem to exact some attempt from it—The importance of Stoney Point to the enemy makes it infinitely desireable that could be the object."[67]

Rather than simultaneously attacking both points, he would hit the tactically more important fort at Stony Point that guarded the west bank of King's Ferry on the Hudson River. That point, a rugged promontory jutting about half a mile into the Hudson, reached an elevation of 150 feet above the river. A deep morass, flooded at high tide, blocked the landward approach to the point. A causeway across the marsh led into the fort and down to the ferry landing. The British had fortified the post with abatis (trees felled in the direction of expected attack with the smaller branches cut off and the larger branches sharpened), redoubts, and detached batteries. The garrison of about six hundred men, commanded by Lt. Col. Henry Johnson, consisted of the 17th British Regiment, the two grenadier companies of the 71st Regiment, some provincial troops, and artillery detachments.[68]

If that assault succeeded, he intended to strike the fort at Verplanck Point as well. He alerted General McDougall to position two brigades for the latter attack.[69] The American commander assigned the attack on Stony Point to Wayne and his light infantry corps. Wayne carried out a reconnaissance of the post and sent a report to

Washington.[70] Washington himself reconnoitered Stony Point on July 6 and gathered information on its strength and the surrounding territory. He decided that the post could only be taken by surprise attack.[71] Washington later explained to Congress his reasons for launching the attack on King's Ferry: "The advantages which the enemy derived from the possession of this post . . . and the inconveniences resulting from it to us" were "sufficient inducements to endeavour to dispossess them—The necessity of doing something to satisfy the expectations of the people and reconcile them to the defensive plan we are obliged to persue, and to the apparent inactivity, which our situation imposes upon us—The value of the acquisition in itself, with respect to the men artillery and stores which composed the garrison—the effect it would have upon the successive operations of the campaign and the check it would give to the depredations of the enemy at the present season: All these motives concurred to determine me to the undertaking."[72]

Washington gave detailed instructions for the attack to Wayne. Giving Wayne leeway to modify the outline if necessary, he gave them as his "general ideas of the plan for a surprise." "It should be attempted by the light Infantry only," he ordered. Secrecy was essential. "As it is in the power of a single deserter to betray the design—defeat the project—& involve the party in difficulties & danger, too much caution cannot be used to conceal the intended enterprise." He gave directions as to the number of men for the attack, the approach route, and the division of the attacking force into a vanguard and a main body. If successful, Wayne should prevent the retreat of the garrison and turn the fort's cannon on Verplanck Point and any British shipping in the Hudson.[73]

Wayne, after another reconnaissance on July 11, decided that "two attacks & one faint" should be made as part of the overall assault. He had, he told Washington, "taken the Liberty to Order Colo. Balls Regimt [of the Virginia troops] stationed at Rose's farm to follow in my Rear." To bolster the morale of his troops, whom he thought would "derive Confidence from the Reputation of Numbers" he planned to give it out that "the Whole Virginia Line are to Support us— it can have no bad Effect—but it may have a very happy one." He had taken precautions "to secure the passes leading to Stoney point" by detaching "three small parties of picked men under Vigilant Officers."[74]

Before marching to make the assault, Wayne issued detailed instructions for the attack to his officers and troops. The instructions also contained some warnings to the troops: "If any Soldier presumes to take his musquet from his Shoulder, or attempts to fire, or begins the battle till ordered by his proper officer, he shall be instantly put to death by the officer next him, for the cowardice and misconduct of one man is not to put the whole in danger, or confusion with impunity. After the troops begin to advance to the works, the stricktest silence must be observed; and the greatest attention paid to the commands of the Officers." But he also included words of encouragement (as well as a final word of warning): "The General has the fullest confidence in the bravery, and fortitude of the Corps he has the happiness to command; the distinguished honor confered on every officer, and soldier who has been drafted into this Corps by his Excellency Genl Washington; the credit of the States they respectively belong to, and their own reputation will be such powerful motives for each man to distinguish himself, that the General cannot have the least doubt of a glorious victory." He promised monetary rewards to the first five soldiers to enter the fort, as well as immediate promotion to the first man to enter. And he pledged to "represent the conduct of every officer and Soldier who distinguishes himself on this occasion in the most favorable point of view to his Excellency, who always receives the greatest pleasure in rewarding merit. But should there be any soldier so lost to every feeling, every sence of honor, as to attempt to retreat one single foot, the officer next him is immediately to put him to death, that he may no longer disgrace the name of a Soldier, or the Corps, or the State to which he belongs." Finally, he declared, "As General Wayne is determined to share the danger of the night, so he wishes to participate of the glory of the day in common with his fellow Soldiers."[75]

At noon on July 15 Wayne and his light infantry began their march from "Sandy beach" about fourteen miles north of Stony Point. "The roads being exceedingly bad and narrow, and having to

pass over high mountains, through deep morasses, and difficult defiles" the troops had to move in a single file for most of the way. By
eight o'clock that night the van of the attack force had arrived within
a mile and a half of the fort. Wayne then formed his assault columns.
Lt. Col. Christian Febiger's regiment of Virginians and Pennsylvani-
ans and Col. Return Jonathan Miegs's regiment of Connecticut men
formed the right column. Col. Richard Butler's regiment of Pennsylvania, Delaware, and Maryland infantry formed the left column. A
detachment under Maj. William Hull of Massachusetts accompanied
the right column and a detachment under Maj. Hardy Murfree of
North Carolina joined the left column. Murfree's men, the only
troops allowed to carry loaded muskets, were to provide a diversion
by keeping up a continual fire once the assaulting troops neared the
works. "The troops remained in this position until several of the principal officers, with myself had returned from reconnoitring the
works." This being completed, at 11:30 at night the assault force
moved to the attack. Wayne assigned as the vanguard of the right
column "One Hundred and Fifty volunteers, properly officered; who
advanced with unloaded musquets and fixed Bayonets under the
command of Lieut. Colo. [Francois Louis de] Fleury; these were pre-
ceded by twenty picked men & a vigilant, & brave officer to remove
the abbatis and other obstructions." Likewise, he assigned as vanguard of the left column "one hundred volunteers, under the command of Major [John] Steward [Stewart] with unloaded musquets,
and fixed bayonets, also preceeded by a brave and determined officer
with twenty men." To support the attack and cover Wayne's retreat,
if needed, Brig. Gen. Peter Muhlenberg took station at the rear of
Wayne's light infantry with 350 men drawn from his brigade.

At midnight, the assault was to have commenced, but the trek
through the "deep morass" in front of the fort, then covered by a
high tide, and the removal of the other obstructions in front of the
fort delayed the attack for twenty minutes. Prior to the assault Wayne
placed himself at the head of Febiger's regiment. He gave his troops
"the most pointed orders not to fire on any account, but place their
whole dependance on the Bayonet." The order, he later reported to
Washington, "was literally & faithfully obeyed." As Wayne described

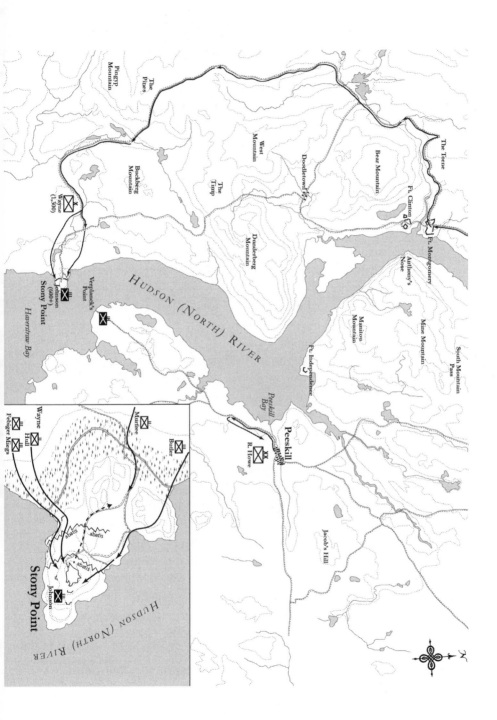

the attack to Washington: "Neither the deep morass, the formidable, and double rows of abbatis, or the strong works in front, and flank could damp the ardour of the troops, who in the face of a most tremendous, and incessant fire of Musquetry, and from Cannon loaded with grape shot forced their way at the point of the bayonet through every obstacle, both columns meeting in the center of the enemies works nearly at the same instant."

The British suffered 63 killed, over 70 wounded, and 543 men captured. Wayne's light infantry sustained only 15 killed and 80 wounded. Wayne himself suffered a wound in the head from a glancing musket ball.[76] In his report to Washington, Wayne, perhaps recalling the British attack at Paoli two years before, when he was surprised by a British bayonet charge that inflicted severe casualties on his brigade,[77] wrote "The humanity of our brave Soldiery who scorned to take the lives of a vanquished foe, calling for mercy reflects the highest honor on them and accounts for the few of the enemy Killed on the occasion."[78]

Having taken the fort, Wayne immediately advised Washington at 2 a.m.: "The fort & Garrison with Colo. Johnston are ours—Our Officers & men behaved like men who are determined to be free." Wayne soon followed this brief note with a letter assuring Washington that the garrison had surrendered and reporting: "It is with infinite satisfaction I acknowledge to you, that the officers, and men under my command behaved with the greatest bravery, and fortitude." He praised Fleury, Stewart, and the other officers who led the vanguard of the attack. He also complimented Butler, Meigs, and Febiger and his other field officers who "acted with that prudent conduct, and calm intrepidity which ever insures success." He acknowledged a special debt to Maj. Henry Lee, commander of a partisan corps, "for the quick and useful intelligence he repeatedly gave me which contributed much to the success of the enterprise." He also praised Lt. Col. Samuel Hay, who was wounded, and his aide-de-camp Henry Walgrave Archer, who "has shewn the Greatest Intrepidity in the Storm."[79]

In hope of exploiting Wayne's attack, Washington directed General McDougall, commanding at West Point, to order down two brigades to attack the fort at Verplanck Point, across the river from

Stony Point. They were to move as soon as McDougall received intelligence that Wayne's attack had succeeded. The attack was less well prepared than the attack on Stony Point. General Robert Howe, commander of the brigades, was ordered to advance to the fort's outer works and open a cannonade against it. "It was hoped, that this might either awe them into a surrender under the impressions of what had happened on the other side or prepare the way for an assault." But the misrouting of Wayne's reports, which Washington had directed to go through McDougall, and delays in bringing up heavy cannon and entrenching tools delayed Howe's attack and he was forced to withdraw when he learned of the approach of a British relief force. "I did not unite the two attacks at the same time and in the same manner, because this would have rendered the enterprise more complex, more liable to suspicion and less likely of success, for want of an exact cooperation, which could hardly have been expected."[80]

Washington came down to Stony Point after the assault to examine the situation. He found that the fort would require more men to garrison it than he could afford without incapacitating his army for other operations. His opinion, backed by his chief engineer and his general officers, was that it would take at least 1,500 men to properly garrison the fort "for its complete defence." The British, depending on their control of the Hudson, had constructed the fort for defense against land attack only. To make the fort defensible would take "a great deal of labour and expence" because the Americans would have to anticipate an attack by water and would have to fully enclose the fort. "While we were doing this, the whole army must have been in the vicinity exposed to the risk of a general action, on terms which it would not be our interest to court, and out of reach to assist in carrying on the fortifications at West Point, or to support them in case of necessity." The "unanimous sentiment," Washington reported to Congress, was to "evacuate the post, remove the cannon and stores and destroy the works." This was completed by the night of July 18.

To British commander in chief General Sir Henry Clinton the attack came as a shock. "My astonishment could not but be extreme when the intelligence was brought me on the 16th that the lines of

Stony Point had been assaulted and carried the night before," he later wrote, "and the guns there [were] playing on Verplanck's, which was likewise menaced by a considerable body of troops in its rear."[81]

Showing the importance he put on Stony Point, Clinton reacted swiftly. As soon as he learned of the fort's fall, he immediately ordered his army at Phillipsburg to advance to Dobb's Ferry with the cavalry and light troops pushed forward to the Croton River "to awe the land operations" of Howe against Verplanck Point. He sent three regiments under a brigadier up the Hudson by boat "with all expedition" to save the Verplanck garrison or recover the fort at Stony Point. Concerned that the troops sailing up the Hudson by a northerly wind and fearing that Washington by that delay might have time to collect a force at King's Ferry too powerful for the detachment, Clinton embarked himself with the light infantry and joined the expedition in Haverstraw Bay. With the bulk of the British army at the ready on the east side of the river, and easily transported to the western shore, he hoped that Washington might be drawn into an engagement.[82] But Washington had suspected such a move and, as we have seen, withdrew.

Even after the war Clinton remained impressed by the American operation: "The success attending this bold and well-combined attempt of the enemy procured very deservedly no small share of reputation and applause to the spirited officer (General Wayne) who conducted it," he wrote in his memoirs, "and was, I must confess, a very great affront to us, the more mortifying since it was unexpected and possibly avoidable."[83]

Washington rightly considered the benefits of the attack "very important." His assessment shows his solid grasp of the strategy of the war: "The diminution of their force by the loss of so many men will be felt in their present circumstances—The artillery and stores will be a valuable acquisition to us, especially in our scarcity of heavy cannon for the forts—The event will have a good effect upon the minds of the people—give our troops greater confidence in themselves and depress the spirits of the enemy proportionably—If they resolve to reestablish the post, they must keep their force collected for the purpose. This will serve to confine their ravages within a narrower compass and to a part of the country already exhausted. They must lose part of the remainder of the campaign in rebuilding the works, and when they have left a garrison for its defence, their main body by being lessened must act with so much the less energy and so much the greater caution."[84] Clinton did in fact have to evacuate King's Ferry to enable his attack on Charleston, launched in December.

Even though Washington had been forced to abandon Stony Point, he continued to consider it the main target for any offensive action by his army, though the defense of West Point remained his overriding objective. He requested that General Putnam, tasked with defense of the Highlands, consult with the generals at West Point and prepare a plan of defense in case of a British move against the critical post.[85] At a council of war, every general agreed that defense of West Point should be the army's primary objective for the campaign; but the generals expressed differing views on the prospects for another attack on King's Ferry, the only offensive operation judged possible without the cooperation of a French fleet.[86]

In August, Washington, expecting another move from Clinton, kept his main army in New York compact and tried to divine British intentions. "The present Æra is big of events," he wrote to one of his generals early that month. "The next ten or twelve days will, most assuredly bring forth something of importance—till which (I mean till the designs of the enemy are a little more unfolded) I shall not think it consistent with military prudence to make further detachments from this army. . . . From Europe, from the West Indies, from the East, & from the west, we may I think look for interesting News—the Military movements in the three last (two of them at least) must have brought matters nearly, to a decision; and from the other that is Europe a few days must discover her views and what is to be apprehended from the long talked of re-inforcement. . . . For sometime past, I have been clear in one of two things, but not decided in either. First that the enemy are really in expectation of a pritty considerable reinforcement with which they mean to take the field and act vigorously, and are in the meantime putting the Island & defences of New Yk in such a situation as to be, with their shipping, held by

a few men—or expecting no re-inforcement & apprehensive of a foreign foe, are preparing for self defence."[87]

As an alternative to another attack on King's Ferry, Washington
decided to attack the less well defended British fort at Paulus Hook,
New Jersey. The defensive works protecting the British outpost at
Paulus Hook were so formidable that most observers thought them
impregnable. Located on the Hudson River directly opposite New
York City, the post occupied a point of low-lying land on a small
peninsula. The British had fortified the point because it lay within
cannon shot of the city.

The main works consisted of a circular redoubt and a fort with
six field pieces, both on high ground. These central fortifications
were surrounded by several blockhouses, one of which protected the
entrance to the post, and breastworks. A double line of felled trees,
or abatis, connected the blockhouses and breastworks. And a battery
and breastwork on high ground protected the southwest, shallow-
water approach to the post. Barracks inside the complex housed the
garrison. A two-mile-wide salt marsh and a tidal creek on the land
approach to the west prevented easy access from that direction. In
addition, the British engineers had added to the landward defenses
by cutting a deep ditch in front of the outer fortifications to extend
the creek's water across the entire landward front, making the fort
an island. The marsh, creek, and ditch made the landward approach
nearly impassable, except at low tide. Only one narrow road crossed
the marsh, with a drawbridge across the ditch.[88] The commander of
the garrison in New York City believed these defenses should have
placed Paulus Hook "out of the Reach of Insult."[89] Perhaps feeling
that these formidable defenses made a surprise attack impossible, the
British command had put only a small garrison of provincials and
second-line troops in the garrison, stiffened by a few regulars. The
garrison consisted of Lt. Col. Abraham Van Buskirk's 4th Battalion
of the New Jersey Volunteers and part of the Royal Garrison Battalion.[90] Maj. William Sutherland, major-commandant of the Royal
Garrison Battalion, was second in command of the Paulus Hook garrison. Washington, General Stirling, and Major Henry Lee, who later
commanded the assault, had been planning this surprise attack since
at least August 10, probably since late July.[91]

Lee was always on the lookout for an opportunity to attack. Despite its formidable defenses, Paulus Hook presented him with one. During his scouting and espionage operations of the summer in support of Wayne's attack on Stony Point, Lee had learned that Paulus Hook "was in a state of negligent security."[92] That, if true, meant the fort could be surprised, if the attack was timed for low tide. Lee may have first broached the idea of an attack on the post in a letter to Washington on July 28. On that date, the general's aide-de-camp Richard Kidder Meade wrote to Lee from headquarters at West Point: "By his Excys desire I wrote to you this morning requesting your attendance here on the very subject mentioned in yr letter of this date—He still requests you will come on after making the necessary inquireys in order that the scheme you propose may be adopted."[93]

During their discussions, Washington gave Lee his general ideas of the manner in which the assault should be conducted and mentioned the precautions that he should take to disguise their intentions and the methods to secure the march of the attacking troops. The general's chief fear was the difficulty of the retreat because of the proximity of Paulus Hook to New York. Washington told Lee that "no time should be lost in case [the attack] succeeded, in attempting to bring off Cannon, Stores or any other article—as a few minutes delay might expose the party, at least to imminent risk." He directed that "no time should be spent in such case in collecting Straglers of the Garrison, who might skulk & hide themselves—lest it should prove fatal." The general added one further stipulation: "if the post could not be carried in an instant by surprise—the attempt must be relinquished." Washington's objective for the attack as he gave it to Lee: "to surprise [the fort]—to bring off the garrison immediately—and to effect a secure retreat."[94] With Washington's tentative approval of the attack, Lee began making preparations, shifting his infantry patrols from the vicinity of Stony Point to the area east of the Hackensack River to cover the area from Bergen and Paulus Hook in the south to Closter in the north.[95]

By August 9, Lee had completed his plan for the attack. On that date, he sent a letter to Washington with plans for the surprise of the fort and the retreat of the attacking force. The commander in chief had reservations. Washington thought Lee's proposal was "well concerted" and "most likely to succeed." But he had doubts, given the strength of the enemy's army at New York, directly opposite the fort. Lee had proposed six hundred men for the attack; Washington rejected that as risking too many. He would only risk three hundred men. The commander in chief suspended the attack as "too hazardous, and not warranted by the magnitude of the object." But he asked Lee to rethink the plan and ordered him to gain information on "such matters as appeared not to be sufficiently well understood," and to report to him on his "opinion as to the probability of success" under a revised plan. Lee quickly reworked his proposal to overcome Washington's objections. He revised his plan to provide for a force of four hundred men, three hundred of whom would be used in the attack. He submitted the new plan on August 11, and the commander in chief conditionally approved it the next day. The general added one defensive precaution: from Fort Lee to Bull's Ferry, all the passes leading from the shore inland were to be blocked with felled trees to hinder the march of any enemy forces that might be landed from the river during Lee's retreat.[96]

Washington gave General Stirling, commander of the Virginia Division, general oversight of the attack, including providing supporting forces. Stirling's division was deployed in northeast New Jersey and thus was the closest to Paulus Hook. Authorizing the attack, the commander in chief directed Stirling to consult with Lee "fully" but gave Stirling the final say in whether they would execute Lee's plan. "Profound secrecy" was to be maintained.[97]

Lee spent the next five days preparing for the assault. Lee personally scouted the approaches to the fort,[98] and he sought intelligence from deserters on the garrison's strength and the fort's internal layout.[99] A report from a deserter placed its strength at four hundred men.[100]

With his own Partisan Corps reinforced by units from the Virginia and Maryland regiments and supported by Stirling's Virginia division, Lee carried out the surprise attack on August 18 and 19. In total, the attacking force consisted of four hundred infantry. Lee divided his force into three columns: a detachment of a hundred Virginians under the command of Maj. Jonathan Clark would compose the right column. Two companies of Marylanders headed by Capt. Levin Handy of the 5th Maryland would form the center column. And a detachment of another hundred Virginians with the light infantry of Lee's corps would compose the left column. To support the attack, Lee planned for one squadron of his Partisan Corps cavalry to take post in the vicinity of Fort Lee and Bull's Ferry with the assignment of observing the movements in the British camps across the Hudson. They were also to alert Lee and Stirling of any British landings on the west bank. Another squadron would secure the roads for the retreat.[101] In addition to the attacking force, Stirling posted a detachment of some five hundred men under the command of Lt. Col. Burgess Ball of the 1st Virginia Regiment at New Bridge to support Lee.

Lee's orders for the attack left no doubt of his resolve. He had, he told his officers, "determined on a universal sacrifice rather than fail." At the conclusion of his orders for the attack, Lee stated his "high confidence" in the "ability, and intrepidity" of his officers and his "certain knowledge" of the "veteranship" of his soldiers. He assured his men that "complete success will and must attend the enterprise." As Wayne had at Stony Point, Lee ordered reliance on the bayonet only: "The columns are to move with muskets loaded—fixed bayonets, pans open—and cocks fallen—No soldier on pain of immediate death to take his musket from his shoulder till ordered—The bayonet to be the only appeal." For inspiration, he asked his soldiers to "recollect and emulate the glorious example exhibited at Stoneypoint on the 16th July." The watch word for the attacking troops, to be echoed at the moment of victory, was "Stoney-Point."[102]

At ten thirty in the morning of August 18, Lee assembled his troops at New Bridge, about fourteen miles from Paulus Hook.[103] About four in the afternoon the troops moved out, crossed the Hackensack River, and moved down the Bergen Road. The marching columns had front and rear guards, as well as flanking parties, all "composed of troops of known fidelity, and directed by officers of vigilance." Patrols of cavalry with "flying parties" of infantry scoured the countryside on the left flank (toward the Hudson) and also in the front and rear of the column. Surprise was paramount. Lee directed the guards and patrols to seize all civilians encountered during the march and commit them to the quarter guard "without respect to age, sex, or character." Lee detached the patrols of cavalry to watch for any British forces crossing the Hudson to reinforce the Paulus Hook garrison or cut his line of retreat. He also stationed small units of infantry to guard the roads leading to the post.

When the assault force moved off the road to cross the mountains, either through "timidity or treachery," Lee's chief guide lost his way, prolonging a short march into one of three hours. His troops were "exceedingly harassed" on this march through the deep woods on the mountain to regain the proper route. Some units in the rear of the column became separated. Referring to his fellow Virginians, Lee later reported to a friend that "near one half of my countrymen left me" at this critical point.[104] Despite Major Clark's efforts to rally them, about a hundred of the Virginia troops, nearly a third of the assault force, abandoned Lee. "This affected me most sensibly," he reported to Washington, not only because of the loss of men but because it "deprived me of the aid of several Officers of distinguished Merit." On the march down the peninsula, Lee dispatched Lt. Michael Rudulph to reconnoiter the conditions at the tidal canal in front of the fort. After a short rest, the troops moved out for the final two-mile approach to the fort. At some point on this march the front, rear, and flank guards were called in.

At a designated point on this final march—a location Lee called "the point of operation"—the officers were to halt the troops and deploy the three assault columns. But now he was late with no time to reorder his attacking forces. Daylight was approaching and the rise of the tide in the river threatened to block the approach route of one unit. Lee explained his command decision at this critical point: "Not a moment being to spare, I paid no attention to the punctilio's of honor or Rank, but ordered the troops to advance in their then disposition." He decided to attack in two columns, instead of the planned three. Clark with the remaining Virginians would attack on the right and Capt. Forsyth of the Partisan Corps would at-

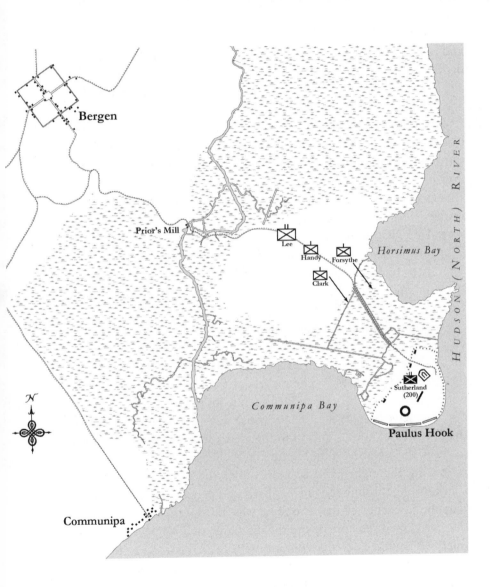

tack on the left. Capt. Handy with his Marylanders would form the reserve.[105]

Shortly after Lee made this critical decision, Rudulph returned and reported that all was quiet inside the fort. He had also tested the depth of the water in the canal and found it high but still fordable. The attacking forces then pushed forward with "resolution, order, and coolness."

Lee was fortunate in the day he chose for the attack. Lieutenant Colonel Buskirk, the commander of the garrison, had marched out the previous evening with a party of about 150 men to surprise what they believed to be a detachment of about 100 American troops assembling in the vicinity of the English Neighborhood and New Bridge. Maj. Gen. James Pattison, commandant of the garrison of New York, had sent forty men from the Hessian Fusilier Regiment Erbprinz under the command of Capt. Henrich Sebastian von Schaller to reinforce the garrison in Buskirk's absence. Thus, the garrison at the time of Lee's assault numbered about two hundred men.[106]

At about three in the morning of the nineteenth the assault commenced. Lee achieved complete surprise. Mistaking Lee's column's for Buskirk's returning detachment, the guard at the post's gate left the drawbridge down.[107] The pickets at the drawbridge, a Hessian noncommissioned officer, and ten men from the Erbprinz Regiment also may have been asleep.[108] The British defenders began firing from the post's blockhouses and from the abatis line, but their fire failed to check the advance of the Continentals. The vanguard troops, supported by the right-hand column under the command of Major Clark, broke through the line of abatis and penetrated to the oblong redoubt. Lee reported that "So rapid was the movement of the troops that we gained the Fort before the discharge of a single peice of Artillery." Captain Forsyth's column, with Lt. Armstrong at the head of the vanguard troops, moved to the left after pushing through the abatis and assaulted the north side of the post. They quickly penetrated to the barracks and captured the officers and troops posted there. Captain Handy's reserve followed the two assault columns into the post. The troops quickly captured the right and center blockhouses, the fort, and the barracks.[109] According to Pattison, the blockhouses were "impregnable except by Cannon" but were "shamefully abandoned" by their defenders.[110] Within the seeming space of only a few moments, most of the post was completely in American hands. Pattison's account gives an idea of the swiftness of the American attack: "Lieut. Cockburne who was the Artillery Officer on Duty there says that a Soldier came to the Hut where He slept, within 30 Yards of the [main] Fort, to give him the Alaerm, that he instantly flew towards the Fort, but found the Enemy Masters of it, whereupon he ran to the Blockhouse, and thereby sav'd himself from being taken Prisoner."[111] The Americans penetrated into the post so quickly that most of the garrison could not be put under arms.[112] Lee's men, however, failed to take the left blockhouse and the round redoubt, in which Major William Sutherland had taken post with twenty-five of the Hessians.[113] The Americans repeatedly called on Sutherland to surrender, but he refused to give up the redoubt.[114]

Before the Americans were in control of the post, Sutherland managed to get a messenger to Pattison in New York requesting reinforcements, and Pattison quickly dispatched the flank companies (one light infantry company and one grenadier company) of the Brigade of Guards, a hundred additional men from the brigade's line companies, and a hundred Hessians under the command of Lt. Col. Cosmo Gordon.[115] But Gordon arrived too late to prevent Lee's retreat.

With a need for a swift retreat, Lee could not bring off the post's artillery. He intended to burn the barracks but found them occupied by sick soldiers and women with young children. The major wanted to blow up the fort's magazine (and also to get some of the ammunition to replace their own wet cartridges),[116] but all attempts to break open the door failed.[117]

The American's belief in the lack of vigilance at the post had been proved correct. The British commander in chief reported that the garrison had been "scandalously absorbed in confidence of their security."[118] One hundred and fifty-eight persons surrendered to Lee's troops. These included seven officers, ten sergeants, one corporal, one hundred and twenty-nine men, and ten "inhabitants," some of whom may have been women.[119] Lee thought he had captured

Sutherland, but on the retreat Lee discovered that the person in the major's uniform was an impostor. In the assault, Lee lost four men killed, three wounded, and seven captured (the last probably stragglers or deserters left behind in the fort as the retreat began). The post's defenders lost, in addition to the captured, ten killed and two wounded.[120]

Though victorious, Lee decided that he must immediately order a retreat. As he explained to Washington: "The appearances of day light, my apprehension least some accident might have befallen the Boats, the numerous difficulties of the Retreat, the harrassed State of the troops, and the destruction of all our ammunition by passing the Canal conspired in influencing me to retire the Moment of Victory." The troops began the retreat about daybreak.[121] Lee assigned Major Clark's column the duty of guarding most of the prisoners and immediately put him in motion. Captain Handy's troops followed, guarding the remainder. Lee formed a rear guard for the retreating columns and placed it under the command of Lieutenants Armstrong and Philip Reid.

He sent a dragoon to notify Stirling that he had begun his retreat. On receiving Lee's report, Stirling pushed forward Lieutenant Colonel Ball's regiment to cover Lee's retreat. Lee sent Capt. Robert Forsyth forward to Prior's Mill with orders to collect the men from the columns most fit for action and take post on the heights of Bergen to cover the retreat.

As Lee and his men marched north in their retreat, British troops closed in on Lee. Advancing on Lee's right flank was Lt. Col. Abraham Van Buskirk's party, which was now returning to Paulus Hook. To his rear was Major Sutherland's. As soon as Gordon's reinforcements were assembled in the fort, Sutherland had taken the light infantry company of the guards, about ninety men, in pursuit of Lee.[122] Arriving at "the point of interception" opposite Weehawken, Lee directed Captain Handy to move with his division on the "mountain road" to "facilitate the retreat." At this critical moment, Capt. Thomas Catlett of the 2nd Virginia Regiment arrived with fifty men ("with good ammunition," Lee noted). The party was part of the Virginia troops that had gotten lost (or abandoned Lee) during the approach march. Lee halted Catlett and detached two parties, one in the Bergen road at the rear of Major Clark's men and one on the banks of the Hudson River. Lee proceeded with the rear guard under Captain Catlett on "the center route."[123] "By these precautions a sudden approach of the Enemy was fully prevented," Lee reported to Washington. About ten miles up the Bergen Road from Paulus Hook, as the rear guard approached the road to the ruins of Fort Lee, Lee's column met Ball's regiment. The colonel moved his force past Lee's column and took up a position to cover Lee's force from any attack.

Shortly after Ball passed Lee, Van Buskirk's force of Loyalists emerged from the woods on Lee's right (north) flank. They moved across the fields toward the Bergen Road and commenced firing on Lee's rear. Lee ordered Lt. Reid to take part of the rear guard troops and engage Van Buskirk. At the same time Lt. Rudulph gathered some men and took post in a stone house, which commanded a bridge across the road. To hinder Buskirk's crossing, the Americans removed the planks from the bridge.[124] The fire from Rudulph's men supported Reid's attack, and together these units bought time for the remainder of Lee's troops to get across English Creek at Liberty Pole (modern-day Englewood, New Jersey). Facing stiff resistance from Lee's rearguard forces and threatened by Ball's superior force, Van Buskirk retreated back into the woods to the north. In this fighting at Liberty Pole, the Americans lost an additional three men captured.[125] Pattison described Van Buskirk's engagement with Lee at Liberty Pole as a "smart skirmish." Although the Loyalist commander suffered no casualties in the skirmish, he was greatly outnumbered by Lee and the approaching Ball. Van Buskirk did not renew his attack and subsequently made his way back to Paulus Hook before dark. Shortly after, Major Sutherland, after pushing ten miles beyond Bergen, abandoned his pursuit of Lee,[126] either due to fatigue (as Lee claimed) or because he observed Ball's force blocking his way to Lee's rear. That evening Pattison withdrew all the reinforcements from the brigade of guards and forty of the Hessians back to New York, leaving sixty Hessians to bolster the defenses.[127] "Thus Sir was every attempt to cut off our Rear completely baffled," Lee reported to Washington. "The troops arrived safe at the New Bridge with all the prisoners about 1 oClock P.M. on the 19th."[128] Lee immediately made a verbal report to Stirling of the success of his attack and Stirling relayed the news to Washington.[129]

Lee received much praise for his leadership in the attack. General Greene believed the enterprise had been conducted with "great spirit" and was "thought to be more gallant than the Stoney Point [assault]." Though the numbers involved were less, because of its proximity to New York and the strength of the fort, "the difficulties were much greater." "The obstacles were so numerous that had not Major Lee been one of [fortune's] favorite Children he must have faild. However he succeeded to the great joy of his friends."[130] Alexander Hamilton called the attack "a handsome stroke." Capt. Samuel Shaw, Brig. Gen. Henry Knox's aide-de-camp, wrote that "The attempt was daring, the difficulties many, the success uncertain, and the retreat, admitting the enterprise to succeed, from the situation of the place and its vicinity to New York, exceedingly precarious." Even his enemies praised Lee. Pattison, as commandant of New York the ultimate commander of the fort, called the enterprise "bold" and said that it succeeded "but too well," given the strength of the post, and that it did "little to the Honor of the Defendants."[131] The commander in chief announced the success of Lee's assault in the general orders of August 22: "The Enterprise was executed with a distinguished degree of Address, Activity and Bravery," the general proclaimed to the army, "and does great honor to Major Lee and to all the officers and men under his command who are requested to accept the General's warmest thanks." After receiving Lee's official report, Washington offered Lee his personal congratulations.[132]

The day after receiving Lee's formal report, Washington forwarded it to Congress with words of praise for Lee and his men. The general informed the delegates: "The Major displayed a remarkable degree of prudence address enterprise and bravery upon this occasion—which does the highest honor to himself and to all the officers and men under his command. The situation of the Post rendered the attempt critical and the success brilliant." He also praised Stirling for "the judicious measures he took to forward the enterprise, and to secure the retreat of the party."[133]

The news of Lee's success helped raise American morale during a difficult campaign.

Although the British retained the post, the capture of another garrison coming so soon after Wayne's exploit at Stony Point greatly embarrassed Clinton. Although he minimized the impact of the attack in his official report, Clinton later complained of Sutherland's misconduct as commandant and disapproved of the verdict of the court that acquitted him.[134]

In the late summer, Washington again exercised the diplomatic aspect of his generalship as commander in chief. When Washington learned that the new French minister in America, the Chevalier de La Luzerne, would be traveling from Boston to Philadelphia, he made plans to receive him at West Point in fitting style.[135]

Washington's three-day meeting at West Point in September 1779 with La Luzerne offers a case study of Washington's executive diplomacy. La Luzerne's secretary, the Marquis de Barbé-Marbois, described their meeting and the trip down the river: "In spite of all the objections of M. de la Luzerne, General Washington came to meet him at Fishkill. He received us with a noble, modest, and gentle urbanity and with that graciousness which seems to be the basis of his character. . . . We embarked with the General on . . . the Hudson, and sailed down it with the tide to West Point where the headquarters are, surrounded by the chief posts of the American army. The general held the tiller, and during a little squall which required skill and practice, proved to us that this work was no less known to him than are other bits of useful knowledge." The dinner that Washington served the Frenchmen became part of his diplomacy. "All the generals and the higher officers were there," Marbois wrote. "It was interesting to see this meeting of these warriors, each of them a patriot renowned for some exploit, and this military meal, served in a tent in the midst of the apparatus of arms, in the heart of the former possessions of our enemies, to a French minister and officers, was to all of us a remarkable novelty. [The general] spoke of the fine behavior of my compatriots and of the glory which they had won in America. . . . A few steps away from us musicians played military and tuneful French airs. The banks and the forests of the mountain answered long to the cannon shots fired to the health of the King and Queen."

The next day Washington, who, Barbé-Marbois noted, "wanted to conduct us himself," led La Luzerne on an inspection of West Point's newly expanded and strengthened fortifications, and the party observed the maneuvers of the army's brigades with Barbé-Marbois commenting on the Continentals: "They had hardly any clothes, but were very well armed, and the men were strong and robust." That afternoon at four o'clock the party dined at the quarters of Brig. Gen. Duportail, Frenchman and chief of the American army's Corps of Engineers. Following the dinner, Washington held a strategic planning conference with La Luzerne.

The American general probed the minister about the possibility of another attempt at an allied offensive in North America. He informed La Luzerne: "That if Count D'Estaing could spare a detachment superior to the enemy's naval force upon this Continent retaining such a force in the West Indies as would put it out of the enemy's power to detach an equal force to this Continent without leaving themselves inferior in the Islands, the measure would have a high probability of many important and perhaps decisive advantages." Washington concluded his remarks at the conference by observing that although with "the great uncertainty of the arrival of a Squadron," he could not begin to "make expensive preparations for co-operating, nor pledge himself for doing it effectually." But, he stated, "there was the greatest prospect of utility from the arrival of such a Squadron." He promised "to do every thing in his power for improving its aid, if it should appear upon our coast" and that "if the present or future circumstances should permit His Excellency Count D'Estaing to concert a combined operation with the troops of these states against the enemy's fleets and armies within these States he would be ready to promote the measure to the utmost of our resources and should have the highest hopes of its success."[136]

At the conclusion of La Luzerne's visit Washington and "the chief officers of his army" escorted him away from West Point and the American commander in chief had two of his generals continue the escort across New York and New Jersey. Showing the effectiveness of Washington's diplomacy, Barbé-Marbois, who himself later became French minister to the United States, commented, "I shall always recall with pleasure the time which I spent with that man who is so much to be respected."

Washington told Lafayette that he had had "great pleasure" in the visit of the two dignitaries. For both, he had "imbibed the most favourable impressions." He continued: "The Chevr till he had announced himself at Congress, did not choose to be received in his public character—If he had, except paying him Military honors, It was not my intention to depart from that plain & simple manner of living which accords with the real Interest & policy of Men struggling under every difficulty for the attainment of the most inestimable blessing of life—Liberty—the chevalier was polite enough to approve my principle, & condescended to appear pleased with our Spartan living—In a word he made us all exceeding happy by his affability and good humour, while he remained in Camp."[137]

Even with his limitations in men, money, and supplies, Washington had sought to take the offensive in the summer of 1779. He had launched a major expedition against the Iroquois that successfully relieved, at least temporarily, the pressure on the western frontiers of New York and Pennsylvania. The American commander in chief had also been able to deliver some sharp strokes in the summer that had embarrassed the British and improved his army's morale. Showing his prudence, he did not fall into the trap of Tryon's Connecticut raid, despite his feelings for the suffering of the inhabitants. Likewise, he wisely realized that he could not hold Stony Point without risking a major action in which he would have been at a great disadvantage. But without naval superiority he had been unable to threaten British control of New York City. In the summer of 1778 and again in 1779 in conferences with Gérard and La Luzerne he had exercised the diplomatic facet of his generalship with great success and proved his readiness to act as the commander in chief of an allied army. His generalship had been prudent yet bold.

Yet Washington was far from satisfied with these limited successes of the summer. When an opportunity arose in the fall to cooperate again with d'Estaing and fulfill the promises just made to La Luzerne, Washington put in motion a campaign to end the war in 1779.

Four

Attack on New York:
The Campaign to End the War

"A glorious object is in view, & God send we may attain it."
—Washington to Benjamin Harrison, October 25, 1779

S IR HENRY CLINTON'S PLANS TO SEIZE THE HUDSON HIGHLANDS
per Germain's plan were frustrated by the late arrival of his reinforcements. Clinton expected the reinforcements to number 6,600
troops. With this sizable addition to his army, as we have seen, Clinton intended to take the offensive and follow up his seizure of King's
Ferry in June by either attacking Washington at West Point or threatening his lines of communication in New Jersey. Clinton's entire plan
of campaign, he later claimed, depended on receiving these reinforcements early in the summer.[1]

Arbuthnot's naval squadron and transports sailed from
Portsmouth, England, on May 1, but he was delayed for a week
countering a French expedition against the island of Jersey.[2] Arbuthnot's ships carried the 76th and 80th British infantry regiments; four
companies of the 82nd Regiment; and recruits and drafts for seven
other regiments, "making in the whole about 3800 men."[3] The
squadron and transports arrived at New York on August 25. Many

of the troops were sick with a "malignant jail fever" that soon infected the New York garrison and put some six thousand of Clinton's troops in hospital. As a result, "I could not look upon this augmentation as adding anything to my strength, " he explained in his memoirs.[4] Clinton later claimed that the unexpectedly small number of reinforcements had forced him to abandon his plans for an offensive against Washington's army.[5]

Since May, Washington had been anticipating the arrival of the British army reinforcements carried by Arbuthnot's fleet. He also had made extensive defensive preparations to counter the offensive he expected Clinton to launch after their arrival at New York.[6] In addition to his preparations discussed in chapter 3, in July Washington directed Maj. Gen. Israel Putnam, commanding the right wing of the army on the west side of the Hudson River, "to consult with the principal Officers, and form a disposition for opposing the *Enemy* in concert, as well in the first instance at landing, as during their progress towards the works [at West Point], in case they should make an attempt upon them." The resulting board of general officers, assembling at Putnam's headquarters on July 22, developed a detailed plan of action for the defense of the West Point forts against all avenues of approach on that side of the river.[7]

By midsummer, Washington had divined Clinton's strategy. He wrote to Maj. Gen. Robert Howe, commanding the forward brigades of the army on the east side of the Hudson River: "If the enemy expect any considerable reinforcement, it is not improbable they are waiting its arrival and will then prosecute their operations on the River, and against the forts [at West Point] that protect its communication."[8] To aid his own thinking—something he often did when considering complex military problems—the American commander wrote out in his own hand a memorandum he labeled "Thoughts on the ways by which West p[oin]t may be attempted by the Enemy." Washington systematically analyzed the several ways he expected the British commander in chief might go about attacking what were certainly his two primary objectives: West Point and the army guarding it. Given the strength of the post's defenses, Washington expected Clinton could only attempt the fortress by surprise or by a regular siege. But he also reasoned that Clinton might try to strike his army without attacking West Point. He analyzed how the British general might carry out either of these operations. Washington concluded the memorandum: "In these cases what is the proper line of Conduct for us to observe? The first great point—is by every possible means to discover the real design of the enemy, & distinguish feints from serious movements. and neglecting the Party intended for the feint unless it can be easily cut of[f] oppose our whole force except what ought to be in the Redoubts to the enemy's which will be found most efficatious upon their flank and rear—in order to gain these it will be necessary if there can be any previous knowledge of the time of their intended movement to advance."[9]

After he received information confirming Arbuthnot's arrival, Washington moved ahead with his final defensive preparations. He proceeded to concentrate the main army to have "the whole army in a condition to operate at the shortest notice & to the greatest advantage."[10] With the exception of Maj. Gen. John Sullivan's brigades on the expedition against the Six Nations, Washington called in his detached regiments.[11] He directed General Howe to put his brigades in a position to join the brigades near West Point on short notice. "The arrival of the enemy's reinforcement renders it necessary to compact our force more than it is at present," he advised Howe. "You will take your measures accordingly. Your movement is to the right so far as to put you in a situation to form a junction with this army with dispatch and without being subject to interruption, under almost any circumstances: this may be effected under the appearances of a forage."[12] He gave directions to Maj. Gen. Stirling to position the Virginia division closer to West Point.[13] He alerted his spies to gather intelligence on the reinforcements and on Clinton's intentions.[14] Washington gave special instructions to Maj. Gen. William Heath, commanding the army's left wing east of the Hudson River:

> That the long expected Fleet is arrived admits of no doubt, though the strength of the re-inforcement is matter of uncertainty. If it is so powerful as to enable the Kings Troops to take the field with a view of meeting this army, Generl Clinton will not, it is to be pre-

sumed, delay the commencement of his operations a moment; because a knowledge of the event must have produced preparatory arrangements for the consequent movements. Under this view & expectation, we also, should neglect nothing by which we can derive any advantage, and as nothing is more essential than a thorough knowledge of ground on which operations offensive or defensive are to be performed, I earnestly desire that you will recommend it to all the Officers under your command (now in the high lands) to make themselves masters not only of the great & leading roads from the enemy's lines, but all bye paths, & even the woods; that defiles may be known & defended to good effect—ambuscades formed—and the Enemys flanks gained with more ease—& if possible unsuspected.[15]

Stating that it was now necessary "for us to double our diligence," he also ordered that Maj. Henry Lee's corps scout and immediately report to him any movement by Clinton.[16]

Washington soon received intelligence that the British reinforcements that had arrived in late August were only half what he had expected and were sickly to boot. The American commander correctly surmised that the British would be unlikely to take the offensive on the Hudson. He began to attempt to determine the British commander's alternative strategy. On September 7, Washington advised Congress that "The current of intelligence from New York makes the late reinforcement under Arburthnot amount to about 3000 troops principally recruits and rather in an unhealthy situation. It also speaks of preparations for an expedition and some recent rumours point to the Southern States, though the enemy have thrown out menaces against this post." He then advised the delegates of his suspicions as to where Clinton would make his next effort. "If the reinforcement does not exceed this estimate they may not think themselves able to operate effectually this way—in which case, the unpromising situation of their affairs may tempt them to make an effort to get hold of some of the southern States, to co[u]nterballance their losses in the West Indies and favor negotiations in the Winter—They have been for some time past fortifying across New York Island; and it is said are going to erect a strong work at Brookline on Long Island: all this may be to have it in their power to secure their present posts with a small force and make large detachments with the greater confidence—A part may go to the West Indies and a considerable number still be spared for the purpose I am supposing—the more so, if Rhode Island, which [is] now become to them a very inferior object should be evacuated."[17]

Fairly certain that Clinton intended no move up the Hudson, Washington informed Howe that he need not move closer to West Point and could keep his division in the eastern part of Westchester County covering the country against any British raid from the sound. He even returned Brig. Gen. John Nixon's brigade, which had been guarding the approaches to West Point below Continental Village, to Howe's division.[18] At about the same time, he received spotty reports that a large French fleet might be on its way to New York.[19] Then, Washington learned that the British had withdrawn several regiments from the King's Ferry garrisons.[20] He began planning for attacks on Stony Point and Verplanck Point with the aid of the expected French fleet.[21] Although he would need reinforcements of militia to conduct large-scale offensive operations, Washington had sizable forces of Continental troops available in mid to late September. In addition to his main army forces (see chapter 3), Washington had two additional corps: Maj. Gen. Horatio Gates's six Continental and five New England state regiments, totaling 2,000 troops, in Rhode Island, and General Sullivan's four brigades with 2,800 men on the march back to the main army after completing a punitive expedition against the Iroquois in western New York. Once Sullivan joined him, Washington's army would number over sixteen thousand men.[22]

In September, then, Washington began turning his mind to his preferred mode of action: offensive operations on a large scale. On September 14, he wrote to General Gates: "I have no official account of any such intended movement in the French Fleet; but I think we ought, at all events, to be prepared for a co operation with them, should they arrive, especially, when it can be done, without deranging our general plan. I would therefore wish you to hold the Continental

Troops, under your command, ready to act as circumstances may require."[23]

The day before penning his missive to Gates, the American commander sent French vice admiral d'Estaing a letter with "hints" for a major allied offensive in the New York City area. He proposed a campaign similar to the second plan devised in May but added a combined attack on the forts at King's Ferry. The general advised d'Estaing that with recently arrived reinforcements he estimated that Clinton now had nearly fifteen thousand men on Manhattan Island and its outlying posts—Long Island, Staten Island, and King's Ferry—in addition to another three or four thousand men at Rhode Island. He informed the admiral of British naval strength at New York and warned him that British commodore George Collier, with a squadron of two heavy and several lighter ships, was still cruising on the Atlantic coast.

After these preliminaries, the American commander outlined a campaign to take all the outlying British forts and garrisons. He proposed that it would be "infinitely interesting" if d'Estaing could use his ships to "intercept"—block the retreat of—the detachments of British troops on Long Island and Staten Island. D'Estaing could also send frigates up the Hudson River. Frigates would also move into Long Island Sound to block the evacuation of the Rhode Island garrison. In conjunction with the French admiral's movement into New York harbor and up the Hudson, Washington's army would attack the King's Ferry forts. His goal was to isolate and capture the garrisons. The American commander made the capture of the forts central to his plans for the offensive. Clearly considering this one of the major operations for d'Estaing's naval force, Washington gave the admiral a detailed plan:

> It will also be of importance to run two or three frigates up the north river into Haverstraw Bay to obstruct the retreat of the garrisons at Kings ferry by water; and I should be happy these frigates may announce themselves by firing a number of guns in quick succession which will put it in my power to push down a body of troops below the garrisons on the East side to intercept a retreat by land to Kings Bridge.[24]

The Continental army would move against the forts on both sides of the river. To block the retreat of the King's Ferry garrisons by land, Washington ordered Wayne and Stirling, on the west side of the Hudson, to position their forces to operate against Stony Point. He ordered Stirling to hold his Virginia Division in "the most perfect readiness" and, as soon as he received intelligence of the arrival of the French (and without waiting for further orders from Washington), to move east toward the Hudson to "intercept" the garrison of Stony Point, cooperating with Wayne's light infantry corps in the operation. The American commander envisioned the operation against Stony Point as a brief siege to capture the garrison, after preventing its retreat by water with French frigates.[25] Howe's division of infantry and cavalry would operate against Verplanck Point to "intercept" its garrison. Washington ordered Howe to march his division to the vicinity of Pine's Bridge on the Croton River. When the French ships appeared in the Hudson, Howe was to move "with all dispatch" to seize the new bridge at the mouth of the Croton "to prevent the escape of the enemy" from Verplanck Point by land.[26] Washington invited d'Estaing to send his own proposals for the campaign "as soon as possible" so the Americans could make preparations "for a perfect co-operation."

The commander in chief concluded with a strong pledge of his determination: "You may depend upon every exertion in my power to promote the success of an enterprise from which such decisive advantages may be expected to the common cause."[27] Though he did not plan to attack New York itself, Washington had nevertheless proposed a bold and ambitious campaign: the capture of all the outlying British detachments.

Why did Washington shift so quickly to an offensive campaign? The arrival of the French fleet offered a solid prospect of the British losing their naval supremacy in the New York area, along with the mobility that went with it. This would be especially true if the British admiral abandoned New York (as he contemplated doing in October when the British received firm intelligence of d'Estaing's arrival on the American coast).[28] The forts at King's Ferry and on Staten Island could no longer be reinforced from New York and would become vulnerable. And as the May conversations with Gérard showed, headquarters had long preferred to take the offensive if d'Estaing came to New York. Brig. Gen. Henry Knox, who as chief of the artillery corps spent much time with the commander in chief, set out reasons for a joint offensive that no doubt reflected the thinking at headquarters:

> An attempt on [New York] in conjunction with a fleet would justify your Excellency in drawing out any number of men and in making the greatest exertions: If it succeeded The Event would amply repay the Expence. If it did not, the very enterprize of reducing the Enemy to stand upon the defence in their Citadel would be such a disgracing circumstance in the Eyes of all Europe and so honorable to our Arms as would fully justify the attempt. Added to which it would totally prevent the possibility of any predatory excursions during the Campaign.[29]

When his further inquiries revealed that d'Estaing was not approaching New York waters, Washington set aside his plan, but he continued to prepare for the fleet's possible arrival, including preparations for attacks on the King's Ferry forts. Washington wrote to Brig. Gen. Anthony Wayne on September 26: "General Knox and Genl du Portail are to go down to night, or early to-morrow to reconnoitre the enemy's post at Stoney point. I have directed them to call upon you. You will be pleased to take proper measures by such a party as you may think necessary to cover them during the execution of their object. The less there is said about this matter the better." On the same day, Washington's aide-de-camp Richard Kidder Meade wrote to General Knox from headquarters: "His Excellency wishes you, in company with Genl Du Portail to reconnoitre the Posts at Verplanks and Stoney Points—His anxiety to have this business entered on immediately induces him to desire you would come down time enough to day, to enable you to take a view of them early in the morning." Knox reported back on September 30 on the results of the reconnaissance.[30]

On September 26, Congress notified the commander in chief that d'Estaing had arrived off the Georgia coast.[31] It seemed that the French admiral intended to execute the second plan agreed to in May (an attack in Georgia followed by a limited operation in New York). Expecting that the admiral would come north to join Washington, they referred "the whole system of co-operation" to the general's direction and authorized him to "concert and execute" any plans with the French he thought proper and to call on the states for any aid in militia and supplies he might require.[32] In short, Congress simply vested the commander in chief with complete power to plan and execute any operations anywhere on the continent with as many men as he could put in the field. Washington received Congress's official report of d'Estaing's arrival on the Georgia coast on October 3. He immediately began to implement his plans for cooperation with the French.[33] The American commander planned for the boldest, most decisive operation he could conceive: an attack on New York City, the bastion of British power in North America.

In a departure from campaigns of previous years, Washington called no councils of war to determine the course of operations. He devised his plan with his aides and input from a few of his senior generals. Stirling and Arthur St. Clair sent detailed operations proposals to the commander in chief in the first week of October. Washington incorporated elements of these, along with previous proposals from other generals, primarily from Wayne, into his campaign plan.[34] His "Thoughts on an Attack of New York," which he wrote out himself, summarized the commander in chief's thinking. In a private letter to St. Clair, the American commander made clear his preference for reserving operational decisions to himself: "I prefer receiving the sentiments of Officers in this way to Councils of War; as I can digest every matter and thing at my leizure, and act with more secrecy than it is possible in pursuance of a determination discovered by a Majority of votes & known to numbers—perusing as I observed before the thoughts of each Officer individually & comparing their reasoning with my own—and forming conclusions which may be secret if necessary."[35]

Now and in the future, the commander in chief alone would decide the operations of the army.[36]

In the first two weeks of October planning and preparing for the attack crowded out all other concerns. Washington gave it his "constant & closest attention."[37] Since September, the American commander's plans for joint action with the French fleet had grown even bolder. His statements leave no doubt that he envisioned a pivotal campaign—what he called "a speedy and decisive effort": an all-out attack on New York, the bastion of British power in North America.[38] He had already informed d'Estaing that he expected "decisive advantages" from the joint campaign.[39] Now, Washington returned to the all-out combined campaign of the May conference. He now envisioned a "decisive stroke"[40] to eliminate *both* of the two largest British forces in North America: the over eighteen thousand troops in and around New York and the four-thousand-man garrison holding the deep-water port at Newport.

Within forty-eight hours of receiving Congress's official notification of d'Estaing's arrival, Washington prepared a lengthy letter to the French admiral with his proposals for the anticipated allied offensive. The American commander would leave the final choice of objective to the French admiral, but he made clear to d'Estaing why New York was his preferred target: "New York is the first and Capital object upon which every other is dependant. The loss of the Army and Fleet there, would be one of the severest blows the English Nation could experience."[41] In addition to attacking New York, Washington proposed that in the three to four weeks it would take for the American militia to assemble d'Estaing should, in conjunction with American troops in Rhode Island, attack and capture the British garrison at Newport.[42] The scope of the operation Washington envisioned required all of his and d'Estaing's troops and all the militia the northern states could raise. He told d'Estaing that "not less than 30,000 Men will in my opinion be adequate to the operation."[43] Of these, the American general, planning to augment his Continentals with over ten thousand militiamen, would supply twenty-five thousand men.[44] A plan on such a scale with the objective of capturing two of the most important centers of British power in North America reflects Washington's aggressiveness. With the prospect of a French fleet to operate with his army, he not only decided on an offensive: he was determined to seek a *major* victory.

Washington's plans would bring all the military and naval power of the allies to bear on New York and its supporting garrisons. The French fleet was essential to the offensive. The general told the officers assigned to meet d'Estaing that the fleet's control of New York waters "must be the basis and Ground work of any co-operation . . . Every thing will absolutely depend upon it." Indeed, without it, Washington would not consider undertaking the combined attack. Gaining naval supremacy at New York appeared to the American commander "the Hinge, the One thing, upon which all Others must rest."[45] The American commander reminded the French admiral that they must strike quickly: "From the advanced Season of the Year, every instant of time is infinitely precious."[46] The French fleet had to destroy or drive off the British squadron. D'Estaing's fleet vastly outnumbered the British squadron at New York.[47] Washington never mentioned the almost certain sea fight that d'Estaing would have to win to gain possession of the harbor. His plans necessarily presumed that the British admiral would abandon New York or that d'Estaing would force his way into the harbor and take control of New York waters; without that no offensive was possible.[48]

The British made preparations to defend New York harbor, but it is doubtful that their efforts would have succeeded if the French had acted aggressively. The British Navy had been caught with only five ships of the line at New York. Vice Admiral Marriot Arbuthnot, commanding the squadron at New York, expressed his "anxiety" regarding how he was to defend New York against d'Estaing's fleet of twenty-five ships of the line.[49] Arbuthnot feared for the safety of his own squadron at New York and for the port of Halifax in Nova Scotia. He was not confident that he could defend the entrance to New York harbor. In other words, the British admiral would have had to try to escape to Halifax or lose his ships—in fact he told Clinton as much[50]—leaving the harbor and the control of the Hudson to the

French, just as Washington planned. In anticipation of the arrival of the French fleet, the British sank hulks near the bar at Sandy Hook, New Jersey, to restrict the ship channel, and they also strengthened the defenses at Governor's Island. The British sinking of hulks in the harbor may have been ineffective; at least Washington received a report to this effect: he told Edmund Pendleton on November 1 that "some unexpected disappointments" had occurred "in sinking their hulks."[51]

The central features of Washington's campaign plan were speed, boldness, and the capture of enemy troops. He intended to take all the British troops in the outlying posts (some seven thousand) with rapid attacks in conjunction with the French fleet and then capture the garrison of New York by siege. The general did not withdraw his more limited proposals of September 13 for attacks on New York's outlying defenses. Instead, he incorporated them into his expanded plans, even sending d'Estaing a copy of his September letter with his new proposals.[52]

The preliminaries of the American general's attack plan involved the French fleet's establishing sea control around New York. He proposed that the French block the evacuation of Newport.[53] By stationing ships in Long Island Sound, the admiral would "cut off all communication between Rhode Isld & New York."[54] He emphasized that it would be "of the utmost consequence to block up the garrison at Rhode Island" and suggested that, for greater surprise, the admiral should detach "a superior sea force" for this purpose before approaching Sandy Hook.[55]

From the memorandum he prepared summarizing his thoughts on the prospective joint offensive, we know that the American general planned for two possible cases: the first, which Washington considered the most desirable, that the British would maintain troops in their outlying garrisons; the second, that they would concentrate their troops in lower Manhattan Island near the city and at Brooklyn on Long Island.[56] Because it would allow him to capture more troops early in the campaign, Washington hoped for the first scenario.

His plans of attack in this case were necessarily the most complex. He intended to quickly capture all the British garrisons in the outlying posts. As already observed, the American commander planned to use the French fleet to take or cut off the Newport garrison. The first part of the plan for the Hudson River region involved the capture of the British troops at King's Ferry and on Staten Island. French warships would "secure the communication" of the Hudson River. If on the appearance of the French the British continued to hold their posts on Staten Island and at King's Ferry, the "first object" of the fleet would be to keep those posts isolated by preventing their evacuation or reinforcement. Washington did not expect d'Estaing to send his entire force into New York harbor—only a "sufficient number" to carry out the blocking operations.

To aid the French fleet's entry into the harbor, the commander in chief gathered pilots and sent them to the New Jersey coast to meet d'Estaing's ships.[57] Washington realized that the services of skilled pilots would be "very essential at the commencement of operations."[58] Perhaps believing that a lack of skilled pilots had been one reason for d'Estaing's reluctance to cross the harbor bar in 1778, he scoured the states of New York, New Jersey, and Connecticut for every pilot he could find familiar with the navigation of New York harbor, the Hudson, and the East River and sent them to meet d'Estaing.[59]

The commander in chief addressed letters to four pilots, informing them that "an event may very soon take place which will render your services of the greatest importance to the public" and urged them to come to headquarters "without delay." Three pilots answered his call.[60] He sent a special request to another pilot, Thomas Hunt (a pilot "intimately acquainted" with the navigation of the treacherous bend in the East River known as Hell Gate), asking for his services and urging him to engage other pilots knowledgeable in the navigation of the waters about New York and in whose "skill and fidelity" he could rely.[61] Hunt soon arrived at headquarters and Washington sent him to meet the fleet. He requested the aid of the governor of New Jersey in locating pilots and sending them forward to meet the French fleet.[62] The general even brought in a pilot specifically to help d'Estaing's frigates negotiate the obstructions the British had placed in the Hudson River channel near Fort Washington.[63]

The American general planned for the allied attacks on King's Ferry to be executed as he had laid out the month before. He told his generals to reposition their forces to prepare for the attacks in accordance with his September orders.[64] He intended for d'Estaing's frigates in the Hudson to "put it out of the power of the detachments to join the main Body."[65] Informing his division commanders on either side of the river that it was of the "utmost importance" to prevent the retreat by land of the British force at King's Ferry, Washington ordered them to position their troops to "intercept" the garrisons.[66] Wayne and Stirling moved their corps to positions near Haverstraw and Kakiat, New York, respectively, in preparation for executing the operation.[67] The American commander wanted the attack on the two points to be sudden. He cautioned Wayne, "I would wish that [they] may be lulled into security rather than alarmed."[68] Howe should take a position near the Croton River that would enable him to reach the new bridge "at the shortest notice" but not so near as to alert the enemy.[69]

The British reacted to Washington's moves against King's Ferry—posts that Clinton wanted to hold to support further offensives up the Hudson. The British commander assembled a task force to counter an attack on the forts. Though he told George Germain, secretary of state for the American colonies, that he believed the American commander's "demonstrations" were not serious, Clinton prepared an expeditionary force of four British and two provincial regiments under Lt. Gen. Charles Cornwallis as a potential relief force for the Stony Point garrison. Clinton himself went by ship to Stony Point on October 11–12.[70]

Washington considered the possession of Staten Island "absolutely necessary" to joint operations against New York. The general proposed to d'Estaing that the admiral "intercept" the detachment on Staten Island as his first task.[71] The commander in chief instructed his envoys sent to meet d'Estaing to "suggest" to the Count that the French "cut off the Enemy's force" on the island "as soon as possible" after passing Sandy Hook.[72] To prevent the retreat of the garrison, the French naval force was to "immediately" destroy all the boats on Staten Island and keep ships in the bay between New York and Staten Island. Washington was sure that these blocking operations against the forts at King's Ferry and on Staten Island would render the "reduction" of the troops at those posts "certain."[73]

But the American commander also planned for direct attacks by American forces against those posts.[74] Even before the official word of d'Estaing's return, Washington had started making preparations for attacking King's Ferry. He positioned Wayne's light infantry corps "to cover the country in the vicinity of Stony Point and to confine the enemy within their works" and directed Stirling to support him with a corps of his division.[75] He ordered Wayne to send parties of light infantry to cover surveys and reconnaissance of Stony Point by artillery chief Knox and chief engineer Duportail.[76] He wanted Wayne to determine if the enemy had bomb-proofs (dugouts with a thick earth and wood covering to make them highly resistant to mortar and howitzer shells, or "bombs"), in the fort, and, if so, "what number, extent, and thickness." Wayne and Col. Rufus Putnam surveyed the fort and determined that it lacked bomb-proofs but had blockhouses.

Washington's generals were confident they could take the forts at the strategically important river crossing. Convinced that he could batter down Stony Point's defenses with five heavy cannon and two eight-inch howitzers, Wayne reported to the commander in chief that his troops could capture the fort's advanced redoubt and "carry the works by storm" after breaches were made by the artillery. Prepared to attack immediately without waiting for cooperation with d'Estaing, Wayne recommended that the army make "a Combined attack" on Verplanck Point at the same time as the assault on Stony Point, as several generals had proposed in July. If the British did not pull out of Stony Point, St. Clair thought two thousand men with "a proper Artillery" could reduce the fort in a week without disturbing "the greater operations of the Army" (the assault on Long Island). The fall of the garrison at Verplanck Point, he thought, "would follow of itself."[77] Wayne was eager to at least bombard the fort, and he thought he could get the British to "move up in force" and "relinquish every other Operation" to reinforce the post. From his scouting of Stony Point ("I have taken a good deal of pains & at some risque," he informed Washington), Wayne provided the American commander with a sketch of the fortifications marked with lines of fire for cannon.[78] Washington also sent Duportail to reconnoiter the British fortifications at Verplanck Point, asking General Heath to provide a covering force for the survey.[79]

Washington also gave thought to preparations for a direct attack on Staten Island. If the allied commanders thought it advisable to "make an attempt" upon the island's forts, the commander in chief thought the following forces could form the attack force: the troops from d'Estaing's fleet (about 4,000); Stirling's division of Continentals (over 1,800) or Wayne's light infantry corps (about 1,200); and the Pennsylvania (1,500) and New Jersey (2,000) militia. Stirling presented the commander in chief with a detailed plan for assaulting the island.[80] Washington promised to give the plan "a proper attention" if they were "fortunate enough to have it in our power to enter upon such an undertaking as your Lordship has supposed."[81]

Because his objective was to capture British troops in the outlying garrisons and prevent them from reinforcing Clinton's other garrisons on Manhattan Island and Long Island, Washington emphasized that these operations should be "speedy," immediate, and "as prompt as possible"; his generals should be ready to move "at the shortest notice."[82] He emphasized to d'Estaing that French ships should "immediately" enter New York harbor to block the movement of British troops by water.[83] The American commander reminded the admiral that "every instant of time is infinitely precious," and that he should "as suddenly as possible" cut off the British garrisons on Staten Island and at King's Ferry.[84] Washington ordered Stirling to have his division in "the most perfect readiness" to "intercept" the garrison of Stony Point. On the approach of d'Estaing's ships Stirling was to move without awaiting further orders from Washington.[85] The commander in chief ordered Howe to have his division ready to block the retreat of the garrison at Verplanck Point "at the shortest notice."[86] He even emphasized to the state executives that "every moment is of infinite value."[87]

With British troops now reduced to those on Long Island and Manhattan Island, the American general planned for main army landings on Manhattan Island and possibly on Long Island. Heath's two divisions west of the Hudson would move south and take a position "in force on the heights above Morrissena." The Continentals and Rhode Island state troops in Gates's division at Rhode Island were to march west and join this force.[88] Washington ordered Gates to hold his regiments in readiness to move by ship through Long Island Sound under convoy of French warships and land at Morrisania, New York, to seize those commanding heights.[89] St. Clair believed that such a move into lower Westchester County would force the British to withdraw to their line of defensive works at Fort Washington on Manhattan Island.[90] Washington planned for these divisions to make feints of a crossing of the East River "to draw the attention of the enemy to long Island & leave that of York more unguarded" while "real preparations are making for throwing Troops over Harlem River." The French would also threaten a landing on Long Island.

Washington planned two landings on Manhattan Island, one with Heath's troops across the Harlem River and one from the Hudson. He designed the attacks to take possession of "the heights above Harlem Plains for the purpose of cutting off the communication & retreat of the Troops from Kings bridge to the City." Protected by French warships in the Hudson and crossing over on boats previously assembled at Stony Point or "some other place least liable to betray the design," troops from Putnam's divisions west of the Hudson would land "at the heights below Harlem plains." St. Clair believed this position "very capable of Defense" and one that would cut off the British in the north of the island from their supplies in the city.[91] D'Estaing's ships would prevent the troops at King's Bridge from crossing the East River to Long Island.

The decision on French and American landings on Long Island, whether as Washington put it "to land in reality, or to make a shew of it," would be contingent "as circumstances may point out and will justify." He proposed that d'Estaing have his embarked troops ready to land on Long Island. St. Clair disagreed with Washington as to the advisability of landing on Manhattan Island. He thought the landing on the island and assaults on the British fortifications there too risky to hazard the army on such an attack. In such an assault, he warned, "the fate of America must in a great measure, be set upon a single cast." He instead proposed a landing on Long Island to capture the heights of Brooklyn. If the allied commanders decided to put an army on Long Island, the American brigades would cross from the vicinity of Morrisania and land at Flushing in the north. The French would land in the south at Jamaica Bay. The allied brigades would join at Bedford and advance on Brooklyn. With the French ships in control of the East River and the allied army now surrounding the forts at Brooklyn Heights, St. Clair believed that "the Post at Brooklyn will soon fall," and "New York, be its Garrison what it will, must fall also."[92] Surprise and deception were essential though. Assuming that they could deceive the British as to their objective and effect a landing on Long Island while most of Clinton's army remained on Manhattan Island, St. Clair thought his plan offered "great probability of success."[93]

Washington's plan for the second case—if the British concentrated near New York City and at Brooklyn—was much simpler. D'Estaing's troops, Stirling's division or the light infantry corps, and the Pennsylvania militia would occupy Staten Island. This force would then be held in readiness "to make a descent at long Island at such a time & at such place as may be agreed on, in order with other Troops which may be thrown across the East River to form an Army for long Island." The remainder of the army would converge on Harlem Heights on Manhattan Island, by way of King's Bridge "if the Garrisons are with drawn" or across Harlem River "if a few Troops are left in [the forts] merely to hold the Works." With French ships guarding the right flank, the army would then advance to "the heights where the enemy had their first lines" and then to "Murrys Hill."[94] Washington appears to have intended this hill, just north of the city, to be the center of the siege line. As the final stage of the offensive in either of the two cases, Washington planned a siege of New York City by "regular approaches."

Intelligence gathering was a crucial component of the commander in chief's plans. He alerted the officers running the American espionage networks on Staten Island to have their spies gather detailed information to support an attack.[95] The general directed Lt. Col. John Taylor of the New Jersey state troops to gather intelligence on the British troop strength and fortifications on the island and send reports "every day or two." As we have seen, Staten Island was to be the campaign's first objective and the general wanted no delay in d'Estaing's landings for lack of intelligence. Washington ordered Taylor to send a report to d'Estaing "at the moment of the Counts arrival."[96] The American commander also ordered Major Henry Lee, stationed with his partisan corps on the coast of Monmouth County, New Jersey, "to be well informed as to the enemy's naval force" at Sandy Hook.[97]

Washington instructed Maj. Benjamin Tallmadge, his officer in charge of the Culper-ring spies in New York City and on Long Island, to have Robert Townsend (alias "Samuel Culper, Jr."), the spy in New York City, obtain information designed to support the campaign. The general wanted "as soon as possible" intelligence "perfectly ascertained" on: the state of provisions in New York; the kind, size, and location of fortifications lately erected on Manhattan Island, Long Island, particularly at Brooklyn; the changes of position of the several British corps; where the enemy ships lay; and if the British were taking measures to secure their shipping.[98] The commander in chief also directed Tallmadge to track British naval movements in Long Island Sound. "It is very interesting at this moment to be well informed of the movements of the enemy's shipping, which may take place in the Sound," he told the major. He ordered Tallmadge to station "an intelligent officer" for the purpose, who was to report every two or three days or "as soon as possible" if any extraordinary appearance of vessels took place.[99]

Also, by October 10, Washington, thanks to his intelligence networks, knew that the long-feared arrival of British army reinforcements, though it had taken place, would not give Clinton the advantage the American commander had feared. His intelligence reports indicated that the 3,800 troops in the reinforcement were "very sickly" and so probably unusable in the winter campaign.[100] In fact, unknown to the American commander, they had infected many of Clinton's other troops. The British commander later stated that six thousand of his troops were sick in hospital during this period.[101] From these intelligence reports, the general knew the weakness of the British naval squadron and the measures the enemy had taken to defend the entry into New York harbor. Washington forwarded all his intelligence reports to d'Estaing.[102]

To increase the effectiveness of his most reliable intelligence network, the commander in chief called a special meeting with Tallmadge to work out detailed instructions for the Culper spies' espionage activities in support of the offensive.[103] After the meeting, he issued detailed instructions for the major to deliver to the Culper spies. Washington gave Tallmadge a list of specific information he wanted from Townsend in addition to "movements by land and Water": on harbor defenses; on the army corps defending Manhattan Island; on the defenses of the island, particularly "whether any works are thrown up on Harlem river near Harlem town, and whether Horn's Hook (the entrance to Harlem creek/Hell Gate) is fortified"; and on supplies and the spirits of "the army Navy and City." Abraham Woodhull ("Samuel Culper"), the spy on Long Island, was to keep his station there as usual to transmit Townsend's intelligence, but Washington gave Tallmadge detailed recommendations for setting up spies to observe the British at Brooklyn, "the only post of consequence, which the enemy will attempt to hold upon Long Island, in case of attack," and the information they were to gather on its defenses. All this intelligence from New York and Brooklyn was "critical." The general recommended "the greatest caution and secrecy" and "no one but the Commander in Chief" was to receive the spies' reports.[104] The scope of Washington's intelligence and espionage activities thus fit the scale of his offensive. And his spy networks delivered quality intelligence to support his planning.

Washington did not underrate the difficulty of such a complex campaign, telling d'Estaing that "the reduction of fourteen thousand Men concentered upon a small Island, with the assistance of Fortifications, is an enterprize of no inconsiderable difficulty."[105] The American commander realized the high stakes involved in such a complicated and difficult, but potentially decisive, operation, and he set these out to the state executives:

On one side—the reputation of our Councils & our Arms and an immediate removal of the War present themselves. on the other, disgrace and disappointment—an accumulation of expence, loss of Credit with our Allies and the World—loss of confidence in ourselves—the exhausting our Magazines and Resources, the precipitated decay of our Currency and the continuance of the War.[106]

Washington felt dissatisfied that he did not have a "definite, preconcerted plan" to act on that would enable him to operate with more "certainty." Nevertheless, he reported to Congress: "I am taking every necessary step for a co-operation, as far as our conjectures of [d'Estaing's] designs, and our situation will authorise."[107] Despite this uncertainty regarding the French admiral's intentions, the American general proposed an all-out attack on New York—a demonstration of his innate aggressiveness as a general. Such a proposal was not the action of a Fabius.

Despite the difficulties of executing such a design, Washington's opponent recognized the decisive potential of such a campaign. Clinton had feared just such an operation in 1777, when General William Howe, then commander in chief, left him to defend New York City. Clinton wrote that if Washington had then seized the heights of Morrisania, landed on the plains of Harlem, and taken Staten Island and Brooklyn, "he could without much difficulty have rendered my hold of New York very precarious."[108]

Washington knew Clinton expected the French fleet and thought Clinton "equally vigorous in preparing for defense."[109] The British had set about strengthening their defensive lines north of the city and at Fort Washington in the northern part of Manhattan Island. They had begun installing extra cannon on Governors Island and constructing new fortifications at Brooklyn. The American commander's spies had informed him fully on these measures.[110] Washington recognized that the British were "providing for the most obstinate resistance," but this he expected: "Indeed as their reduction [the surrender of New York and its garrisons] would be attended with the most alarming and fatal consequences to their Nation, nothing else can be reasonably expected."[111]

To achieve his pivotal victory Washington made preparations to use all the resources of the continent. In a joint campaign with the French, "it will be incumbent upon us to exert our utmost resources," he told New York governor George Clinton on September 27.[112] The general concentrated the Continental army, calling in most of his outlying brigades and regiments. He urged Sullivan to hurry the return of his brigades "with all possible dispatch." He ordered Col. Moses Hazen to march his 2nd Canadian Regiment from New Hampshire to join Howe's division south of the Croton River. And he recalled the North Carolina brigade from its march to South Carolina.[113] To augment the Continental army, the American commander called on the five states nearest the anticipated scene of operations to provide a total of twelve thousand militiamen "properly equipped" to serve for three months, a force which he deemed "indispensible" to the operation. Massachusetts was to provide 2,000; Connecticut, 4,000; New York, 2,500; New Jersey, 2,000; and Pennsylvania, 1,500 militiamen.[114]

The great offensive would necessarily demand the use of all available resources and supplies. In response to a letter from Washington asking that he make ready transportation and equipment to support the joint campaign, Quartermaster General Nathanael Greene advised the commander in chief of the difficulties he expected, largely from a lack of money, but ended his letter with this optimistic opinion: "Nevertheless such an enterprize will give great spirits to the Country and engage their whole force to assist the Army. I think we may expect upon such an attempt (as is proposd) double the assistance which could be had upon ordinary ocasions."[115]

Washington's marshaling of resources fit the scale of his conceived operations. He wanted Greene prepared for "the whole Army's" moving "upon the shortest Notice." "Our move, if we make one in consequence of the Counts arrival," he informed the quartermaster general, "will most probably be downwards, with the greatest part of the Army."[116] With d'Estaing's arrival imminent, Greene must have boats, tents, and wagon teams made ready "as soon as possible" to support the allied operation.[117] For the final phase of the attack siege equipment would be important. The commander in chief ordered the

Connecticut militia regiments on station in the west of that state to construct fascines and gabions, equipment "very important to our measures," and store them at a spot safe from the enemy. The general even assigned a French engineer to supervise the effort.[118] Washington did not overlook clothing. He issued this urgent order to Clothier General James Wilkinson: "I request that you will use every practicable exertion to have All the Coats—Waistcoats—Breeches—Blankets Woollen Overalls—Shirts—Shoes—Stockings—Hats—Caps—Watchcoats & Woollen Mitts—belonging to the Continent, brought on to Newburg [just north of West Point] without a moment's delay. The exigency of our Affairs demands it."[119] Food supplies also received the commander in chief's attention. He directed Commissary General Jeremiah Wadsworth to "immediately pursue every measure in your power for providing supplies and stores of provision" for the combined offensive, including supplying "a considerable body of Militia."[120] Stating that it was "indispensible to our measures," he ordered Wadsworth to lay in large supplies of ship bread and rum.[121] The army was short of flour but had an ample supply of meat.[122]

Washington realized that his campaign plan would require "the calling out all the resources of the Neighboring States."[123] Informing them that the "emergency is pressing," the American commander called on the states for food and transportation.[124] He requested powder supplies from Connecticut and Massachusetts to make up Continental deficiencies.[125] The general acknowledged the difficulties of meeting his calls for support, but he was convinced the states would rise to the crisis:

> These difficulties were sufficient to deter me from the plan I mean to pursue, were I not convinced that the magnitude of the object will call forth all the Vigor of the States and inspire the people with a disposition to second the plans of their Governors, and give efficacy to the measures they adopt. I doubt not our resources will be found fully adequate to the undertaking if they are properly exerted—and when I consider the delicacy of the Crisis—and the importance of the object to be attained—I cannot doubt that this will be the case.[126]

The states, in fact, responded generously, meeting almost all of Washington's requisitions for men and supplies. Pledging a "prompt & full compliance" with his request for militiamen, New York governor George Clinton assured the general that his state would "adopt the most vigorous measures."[127] By late October, Massachusetts and New York put their requested militia in the field and Connecticut had its militiamen ready and standing by to march.[128] New Jersey began raising its quota.[129] The Massachusetts council ordered a hundred barrels of powder sent to the Continental army and Connecticut agreed to supply the army with ten to fifteen tons of powder.[130] New Jersey passed an act to supply the army with flour.[131] New York required its militiamen to bring their own forty-day supply of flour and additionally pledged a "competent supply" of flour for the main army.[132] With such a marshaling of resources Washington could truly report to Lafayette: "We are making every preparation in our power, for an extensive and perfect co-operation with the Fleet."[133]

With such a commitment of resources on such a scale, Washington did not just intend to win a victory; a close examination of his writings reveals that he intended to end the war. Three days after laying out his plan to d'Estaing, the American commander made his most forceful appeal for decisive, joint action. During a visit to West Point the outgoing French minister Gérard appears to have informed Washington that d'Estaing might not have time for a complicated operation against New York. The admiral would bring his fleet to the Capes of Delaware for supplies and then decide on his next operation, probably against Halifax.[134] The general did not retreat from his plan. Instead, this information prompted his boldest appeal to the French admiral: the passage quoted at the beginning of the introduction.[135] Such a bold statement, committing the entire Continental army and the maximum resources in militiamen and supplies from five states to a campaign involving great risks begs the question: why did Washington's strategy shift so rapidly from the limited allied offensive agreed upon with Gérard in May and which he proposed to d'Estaing in September to a decisive, all-out allied offensive against

New York (an operation that by his own admission would put "much to the hazard"?)[136]

Though Washington never explicitly stated his reasons, one can surmise his reasoning from his statements during this period. First, he rightly considered New York the most important strategic objective, because if a campaign against New York succeeded, "it would be decisive" with the potential to end the war in the states.[137] The loss of such a number of troops, over eighteen thousand (twenty-two thousand if the troops at Newport were also captured) would indeed have been pivotal: Great Britain, even with her great wealth, could not replace that many troops; it would, as Washington pointed out to d'Estaing, be the severest blow they could deliver. He also knew his regiments would never be stronger than in the fall of 1779: many enlistments were expiring at the end of the year and recruiting was going slowly.

Third, Washington doubted the states' ability to sustain the war beyond 1779. He feared the impact on the army of the rapidly depreciating currency, which he called the "great impediment to all vigorous measures."[138] The country's affairs, he confessed to New York congressman Gouverneur Morris shortly after his meeting with Gérard in May, were in a "very disagreeable train."

> The rapid decay of our currency, the extinction of the public spirit—the increasing rapacity of the times, the want of harmony in our councils—the declining zeal of the people—the discontents and distresses of the officers of the army—and I may add the prevailing security and insensibility to danger—are symptoms in my eye of a most alarming nature.[139]

The general had feared the people's loss of virtue and the decline in revolutionary spirit since late in 1778. He had complained to Pennsylvania governor Joseph Reed in December 1778 of the "murderers of our cause—the Monopolizers—forestallers—& Engrossers," men Washington called the "pests of Society" and "the greatest enemies we have." Writing to Virginia assemblyman Benjamin Harrison in the same month, Washington observed that "our Affairs are in a more distressed, ruinous—& deplorable condition than they have been in Since the commencement of the War." He was "alarmed" and wished to see his countrymen "roused." He confessed "that I feel more real distress on acct of the present appearances of things than I have done at any one time since the commencement of the dispute."[140]

Finally, the American commander may have felt France demanded and expected a decisive campaign. Congress had recently notified the states of French dissatisfaction with their efforts. John Jay, president of Congress, sent the commander in chief a copy of the letter. "It is proper you should be informed that our allies were much concerned to find that preparations were not earlier made for a vigorous campaign," the delegates declared to the state governments. "The exertions of America are necessary to obtain the great objects of the alliance, her liberty, sovereignty and independence." Congress urged the states "to prepare for the most immediate and most vigorous operations" by filling up their Continental regiments and having their militia "ready to march at the shortest warning." It was, Congress said, "highly probable that circumstances may soon call them forth to operate offensively and it is hoped and expected with such energy and effect as to free these States from their hostile invaders."[141]

In short, Washington had become persuaded that the moment had arrived for a major campaign *to end the war*. In a letter urging Sullivan to speed his army's return to the Hudson, the commander in chief asserted that this juncture "may be the most important that America has seen during this war." He was, he told Sullivan, planning a decisive campaign "that a period may be put to the hostilities of the enemy in these states."[142] And when Gates wrote Washington that he understood "the Greatness of Your Designs" and that he perceived that "you mean by one Great Stroke to Finish the War," the commander in chief did not refute that characterization of his goal.[143] Interestingly, General Clinton, probably the ablest British strategist of the war, shared Washington's view of the decisive importance of New York. In 1777, while commenting on British strategy for that year's campaign, Clinton had remarked that "it was worth Washington's while to risk everything to get [New York]; . . . by it he finished the *war*."[144]

As the fall advanced with no sign of d'Estaing's fleet at New York, Washington became doubtful but still hopeful. His letter to Benjamin Harrison of October 25, 1779:

> We are now, in appearance, launching into a wide and bound-less field—puzzled with mazes and o'erspread with difficulties—a glorious object is in view, & God send we may attain it—sometime ago it was much within the reach of probability; but the Season—and the incessant labour of the enemy to secure the City & harbour of New York are much opposed to us, & serve to lessen my hopes in proportion as time rolls on. It is now 30 days since Congress gave me official notice of Count D'Estaings intended co-operation, & no authentic acct of him is since come to hand—The probability therefore is, that we shall have hot work in a cold season.
>
> I have called upon Massachusetts bay—Connecticut—New York—New Jersey—& Pensa for Militia—and every thing being in a proper train for a capitol enterprize, to the Gods & our best endeavours the event is committed.

By the beginning of November, with all his preparations for the attack "done, and doing," Washington could only await d'Estaing.[145] As early as October 20, he had begun to fear that d'Estaing's tardiness might affect the success of the campaign. The general confessed his "impatience and anxiety" to Lafayette.[146] He succinctly summarized his situation to an old friend: "To Count D'Estaing then, and that good Providence w[hi]ch has so remarkably aided us in all our difficulties, the rest is committed."[147] By November 10, the American commander had become frustrated with the Frenchman's failure to appear. "There seems to be the strangest fatality, & the most unaccountable silence attending the operations to the Southward that can be conceiv'd," he complained to his wife's son. "Every measure in this quarter is hung in the most disagreeable state of suspense." "Despair" and "uncertainty" were "succeeding fast to the flattering ideas we but lately possessed."[148] Four days later, he asked Congress for authorization to terminate his preparations for the cooperation, and on November 16 he declared all prospects for joint operations with d'Estaing "at an end."[149] The French commander's campaign against Savannah, in fact, had failed in early October and instead of sailing to New York he had returned to France with part of his fleet, sending the remainder back to the West Indies.

Yet, while the prospect of naval supremacy had existed and he had felt the object justified the risk, Washington had not hesitated to form an audacious campaign plan designed to end the war. And it is important to remember that Washington was not just planning an offensive: his preparations were in motion; he fully intended to carry out the attack.

But he was not necessarily wedded to his own plan. When General Duportail and Lt. Col. Alexander Hamilton, Washington's aide-de-camp, sent by the general to meet d'Estaing, suggested that the Frenchman might not desire to undertake the extensive operations he had proposed, the commander in chief authorized the officers "to engage the whole force described in my letters to him, comprehending the continental troops and militia, in such an enterprise against the enemy's shipping, as the Count and you may agree to undertake. *In a word, I will aid him, in every plan of operations against the enemy at New-York, or Rhode Island, in the most effectual manner, that our strength and resources will admit.* He has nothing more to do, therefore, than to propose his own plan, if time will not permit him to accede to ours; weighing thoroughly the consequences of expence and disappointment."[150]

Washington thus made clear that his goal was to strike an important blow and gather fruit from the alliance while he had naval superiority, and, notably, he left the final decision on what operation to execute up to his ally. This would continue to be his strategy over the course of the next two years whenever the prospect of operating with a French fleet arose—an important point most historians have overlooked.

Although d'Estaing did not bring his fleet to New York and Washington could not execute the great offensive, the campaign season bore fruit nevertheless. First, the threat of a combined offensive against New York kept Clinton on the defensive for three months. Second, the British decided to evacuate King's Ferry. Sir Henry had decided that he could not hold the strategically important river crossing during the winter and still provide sufficient regiments for a campaign in South Carolina. By October 21, Washington had intelligence that Clinton was evacuating his outlying garrisons at King's Ferry and Newport and concentrating his whole force at New York.[151] The British evacuated Stony Point and Verplanck Point on October 20 and 21. Although not a direct result of allied operations, Clinton's retreat from the King's Ferry forts, which Washington quickly reoccupied and refortified, bore important strategic fruit. It eased the American general's supply situation and strengthened his hold on West Point.[152]

But by far the most important reaction to the threat of joint operations between the Continental army and the French fleet—and the major fruit of the campaign—was the British army's abandonment of Newport on October 25. In what was perhaps one of the most colossal blunders of the war, Admiral Arbuthnot had insisted on evacuating Newport to make the job of his small naval squadron easier. Then, thinking the deep-water port might be useful if Halifax fell to the French, he changed his mind. But Clinton received word of Arbuthnot's reversal too late and evacuated the port. Clinton planned to use the troops for his southern offensive. The evacuation had important strategic consequences. In 1780 Newport became the base for a French fleet and expeditionary army that eventually helped Washington take Yorktown.[153] Washington even saw advantages in the reverse at Savannah: "The failure of our attempt to the Southward is by no means as disagreeable as represented," he declared to General Wayne. "Altho' we were repulsed in the storm of the works of Savannah, we met with no opposition afterwards in removing our stores and baggage. A number of successes both at Sea and land, have greatly crumbled the enemys force in this quarter. The allied men and officers harmonised perfectly, and behaved with great bravery on the occasion. It would appear that there was an absolute necessity for the Counts returning to the West Indies."[154] He wrote along similar lines to General Lincoln: "I had the mortification of hearing of the

ill success of the allied Arms before Savannah. While I regret the misfortune, I feel a very sensible pleasure in contemplating the gallant
behaviour of the Officers and Men of the French and American
Army, and it adds not a little to my consolation, in learning, that, instead of the mutual reproaches which too often follow the failure of
enterprizes depending upon the cooperation of troops of different
nations, their confidence in and esteem for each other is increased. I
am happy in beleiving that the delicacy and propriety of your conduct, upon every occasion, has contributed much to this agreeable
circumstance."[155]

In planning and preparing for what he hoped would be the decisive
offensive of the war, Washington demonstrated decision, boldness,
and thoroughness. When the promise of naval superiority beckoned,
he immediately seized the opportunity to take the offensive. The hall-
marks of his generalship were *rapid decision making, detailed planning, and thorough preparation.* His correspondence shows the
rapidity and extent of the commander in chief's planning. Within
days of receiving intelligence that d'Estaing might be returning to the
continent from the West Indies, Washington began moving his corps
and divisions, advising governors of potential calls for militia, and
making logistical arrangements. When Congress advised him to expect d'Estaing to come to New York and ordered him to plan and
execute combined operations, the American commander was ready
within two days to send d'Estaing his detailed plan of operations. He
then intensified preparations in a multitude of areas. If indecision
had ever been a characteristic of Washington's generalship, it was no
longer.

With all prospect for offensive action at an end, the American
commander began preparations to move the army into its winter en-
campments. To reinforce the southern theater, where Clinton's next
attack was expected, he ordered the Virginia and North Carolina
troops to march for South Carolina.[156] Washington advised Congress
of his plans. "I am now using my best endeavours to get things in
train for putting the Army in quarters," he wrote on November 24.

With winter coming on his thoughts also turned to getting proper clothing for his men:

The distribution of Cloathing, owing to it's late arrival—the scantiness of the stock—the diversity in colour and in quality—its not having been properly assorted when packed—the absence of Cloathiers under various pretences, for getting Articles that would be deficient &c., has proved a matter of the most irksome delay and difficulty. Owing to these causes and Two Rainy days, the North Carolina Troops could not move from Windsor till Yesterday, notwithstanding the most active exertions of Colo. Clarke, who commands them—and all parties engaged to effect it. I hope however that what cloathing was here and to be distributed here will be so delivered by to morrow evening—that all Troops except those intended for the Garrison [of West Point] will be able to move towards the places designed for their cantonment, without more delay. In fixing on these, we are obliged to regard in a particular manner—the security of this post [West Point]—the security of the Army—the best protection circumstances will admit of to the Country—our supplies of provision and Forage—and the means of transportation. From the fullest consideration of the point, it appears that these Objects in a combined view, will be best answered, by quartering the Cavalry in Connecticut—a Brigade at Danbury—a Sufficient Garrison here including the posts at King's ferry & the Continental village, to secure them, at least against any sudden attempts on the part of the Enemy—A Small body of Troops at the entrance of the Clove and the Main body of the Army in the Country in the Neighbourhood of Scot's plains [in New Jersey], if the circumstances of wood and Water will admit. The Qr Master General and Other Officers are now advanced & employed & have been for some days, in reconoitring a proper position. The instant matters will permit—I shall go forward myself.[157]

Washington also took time to assess his enemy at the end of the fourth year of the war. The British conduct of the war continued to baffle him. To a friend he wrote:

It may not be amiss to observe, that excepting the plundering expedition to Virginia, and the burning one in Connecticut the enemy have wasted another Campaign (—till this stage of it at least) in their ship-bound Islands—and strongholds, without doing a single thing advancive of the end in view, unless by delays & placing their whole dependance in the depreciation of our money, & the wretched management of our finances, they expect to accomplish it.

In the meanwhile they have suffered—I do not know what other term to give it—a third part of the Continental Troops wch altogether was inferior to theirs, to be employed in the total destruction of all the Country inhabited by the hostile tribes of the Six Nations—their good & faithful Allies! while the other two thirds without calling upon the Militia for the aid of a single man excepting upon the Inhabitants in the vicinity of this Post (& that for a few days only) at the time Genl Clinton moved up the River in the spring & before we could reach it—restrained their foraging parties, confined them within very circumscribed bounds at the same time bestowing an immensity of labour on this Post—more important to us, considered in all its consequences—than any other in America.

There is something so truely unaccountable in all this that I do not know how to reconcile it with their own views, or to any principle of common sense—but the fact is nevertheless true.[158]

And to one of his generals who would have had a large part in the offensive against New York he took an even wider view of the scene at the end of the year. America, he believed, was "essential to the existance of Great Britain as a powerful Nation." He thought "her fallen state" was a consequence of Great Britain's separation from the United States. "It was of magnitude sufficient to have made a wise & just people look before they leaped." He argued that "Public virtue—public œconomy—and public union in her grand Council" had disappeared from Great Britain. "Stock jobbing, speculation dissipation luxury & venality with all their concomitants are too deeply rooted to yield to virtue & the public good," he continued.

"We that are not yet hackneyed in vice—but infants as it were in the arts of corruption—& the knowledge of taking advantage of public necessity (tho' I am much mistaken if we shall not soon become very great adepts at them)—find it almost, if not quite impossible to preserve virtue enough to keep the body politic & corporate in tolerable tune—It is scarcely to be expected therefore that a people who have reduced these things to a system & have actually interwoven them into their constitution should at once become immaculate." He then turned back to the war and his disgust at the way he perceived the British had conducted it in 1779:

I do not know which rises highest—my indignation or contempt for the Sentiments which pervade the Ministerial writings of this day—these hireling scriblers labour to describe & prove the ingratitude of America in not breaking faith with France—& returning to her Allegiance to the Crown of Great Britain after its having offered such advantageous terms of accomodation—Such Sentiments as the[s]e are insulting to common sense & affrontive to every principle of sound policy & common honesty. Why has She offered these terms? because after a bloody contest, carried on with unrelenting & savage fury on her part the issue (which was somewhat doubtful while we stood alone) is now become certain by the aid we derive from our Alliance—notwithstanding the manifest advantages of which, and the blood and treasure which has been spent to resist a tyranny which was unremitted as long as there remained a hope of subjugation we are told with an effrontery altogether unparrallelled that every cause of complaint is now done away by the generous offers of a tender parent—that it is ungrateful in us not to accept the proffered terms—and impolitic not to abandon a power (dangerous I confess to her but) which held out a saving hand to us in the hour of our distress— What epithet does such Sentiment merit? How much shd a people possessed of them be despised? From my Soul I abhor them! A Manly struggle, had it been conducted upon liberal ground—an honest confession that they were unequal to conquest—& wished for our friendship, would have had its proper weight—but their cruelties, exercised upon those who have fallen within their power—the wanton depredations committed by themselves and their faithful Allies the Indians—their low & dirty practices of Counterfeiting our money—forging letters—& condescending to adopt such arts as the meanest villain in private life would blush at being charged with has made me their fixed enemy.[159]

When he penned these words, Washington's war in 1779, at least in its active operations, was at an end. Although he had not been able to end the war as he had hoped, he had moved closer to that goal, perhaps closer than he realized.

CONCLUSION

The Evolution of a General

IN THE FALL OF 1779, WASHINGTON PLANNED HIS BOLDEST campaign. His plans for the great offensive against the British in New York show him as an active and confident commander in chief designing a decisive allied campaign against the main bastion of British military power in North America. When the prospect of the arrival of a powerful French fleet to aid his Continental army emerged he opted for a knock-out punch. His campaign plan reveals the commander in chief's aggressiveness and decisiveness when the opportunity for a war-winning battle presented itself. The plan, although on a much larger scale than earlier offensives in 1779, fit the pattern of his operations that year. There was no "forgotten war" in 1779 and Washington was certainly not in a "limbo of inaction." He sought to deliver all *possible* blows: Sullivan's expedition, Stony Point, Paulus Hook, and then, when naval superiority appeared possible, an attack with the whole Continental army on New York. All this reveals Washington to be an aggressive general: not the Fabius of legend. He knew the need to keep the Continental army from destruction, but he was fully prepared to risk it in operations that promised a *decisive* victory that *could end the war*.

In the year and a half between the Battle of Monmouth in June 1778 and the close of the campaign of 1779, Washington had evolved from an army commander to the general of an army prepared to conduct operations on a continental scale. Congress's vote of confidence in him as commander in chief had been crucial to enabling that evolution, but it had been his own command of strategy and all the affairs of the army that had prompted that vote of confidence. He began the year with Congress growing to trust him to determine strategy, give him command of all theaters, carry out operations as he saw fit, and conduct joint operations with the French. He moved forward to plan an offensive against the chief post of Great Britain's military power in North America. By the end of the year, despite d'Estaing's failure to appear at New York, Washington had fulfilled Congress's trust. He had become truly commander in chief of the Continental army. He acted as army commander, diplomat, strategist, administrator, planner, and organizer. Congress vested him with great military powers, and he fully justified their confidence in him. The campaign of 1779 culminated with Washington conducting preparations for a major combined French and American attack on New York in which Washington demonstrated all those facets of his generalship. In the years to come the experience gained in this year would prove vital to Washington's command of the army and his role as allied commander in chief. Although he had been prevented from carrying out the decisive, war-winning attack he desired, Washington had nevertheless demonstrated the potential of what he could achieve when supported by a French fleet and army. In the following two years, with the arrival of another fleet and army from France, he would fulfill that potential. Using all he had learned in 1779, Washington would take that allied army to a small town on the banks of the York River in Virginia—Yorktown—and win the decisive victory that eluded him in 1779.

NOTES

ABBREVIATIONS

JCC: *Journals of the Continental Congress.*
PGWRW: *The Papers of George Washington. Revolutionary War Series.*
NHi: New-York Historical Society.

CHAPTER ONE: A NEW WAR

1. Mark Edward Lender, "The Politics of Battle: Washington, the Army, and the Monmouth Campaign" in Edward G. Lengel, ed., *A Companion to George Washington* (Malden, MA: Wiley-Blackwell, 2012), 227, 243. Lender's argument that Monmouth was more a political victory for Washington than a tactical victory and that the battle solidified his position as the army's general is persuasive. See also Lender and Gary Wheeler Stone, *Fatal Sunday: George Washington, the Monmouth Campaign, and the Politics of Battle* (Norman: University of Oklahoma Press, 2016), 382-403, 424-25.

2. Jonathan R. Dull, *The French Navy and American Independence: A Study of Arms and Diplomacy*, 1774-1787 (Princeton: Princeton University Press, 1975), 112.

3. Henry Laurens to GW, July 10, 1778, *PGWRW*, 16:45-46.

4. Henry Laurens to GW, July 14, 1778, *PGWRW*, 16:74-75; GW to d'Estaing, July 17, 1778, *PGWRW*, 16:89-91.

5. Henry Laurens to GW, 11 July 1778, *PGWRW*, 16:56-57.

6. The exact language of the resolution was: "it is the desire of Congress that [Washington] co-operate with his excellency Count d'Estaing ... in the execution of such offensive operations against the enemy as they shall mutually approve." JCC 11:684.

7. GW to d'Estaing, July 14, 1778, *PGWRW*, 16:67-71.

8. D'Estaing to GW, July 8, 1778, *PGWRW*, 16:38-39.

9. D'Estaing to GW, July 13, 1778, *PGWRW*, 16:63.

10. GW to d'Estaing, July 17, *PGWRW*, 16:88-89.

11. GW to Gates, July 14, 1778, *PGWRW*, 16:71-72.

12. GW to Jonathan Trumbull, Sr., July 14, 1778, *PGWRW*, 16:76-77.

13. D'Estaing to GW, July 17, 1778, *PGWRW*, 16:89-90.

14. GW to Maj. Gen. John Sullivan, July 17, 1778, *PGWRW*, 16:92-94.

15. GW to Maj. Gen. John Sullivan, July 17, 1778, *PGWRW*, 16:92-94.

16. Hamilton to GW, July 20, 1778, *PGWRW*, 16:109-110.

17. "General Orders," July 22, 1778; GW to Lafayette, July 22, 1778; and "Council of War," July 25, 1778, *PGWRW*, 16:121-23, 127, 160-64.

18. GW to d'Estaing, July 22, 1778, *PGWRW*, 16:125-26.

19. GW to Lafayette and to Sullivan, both July 27, 1778, *PGWRW*, 16:185-88.
20. For a full account of the Rhode Island campaign, see Christian M. McBurney, *The Rhode Island Campaign: The First French and American Operation in the Revolutionary War* (Yardley, PA: Westholme Publishing, 2011).
21. GW to John Sullivan, July 27, 1778, *PGWRW*, 16:187-88.
22. Lafayette to GW, August 25-26, *PGWRW*, 16:369-75.
23. Sullivan to GW, August 23, 1778, n.1 in *PGWRW*, 16:360-61; Lafayette to GW, August 25-26, 1778 n.4, in *PGWRW*, 16:374; GW to Greene, September 1, 1778, *PGWRW* 16:458-59; GW to Lafayette, September 1, 1778 (second letter), *PGWRW* 16:461-64; and John Laurens to GW, September 2, 1778, *PGWRW* 16:479-80.
24. Lafayette to GW, August 25-26, 1778, *PGWRW*, 16:369-75; and Lafayette to GW, September 1, 1778, *PGWRW*, 16:461-64.
25. GW to Nathanael Greene, September 1, 1778, in *PGWRW*, 16:458-59.
26. GW to William Heath, 28 Aug. 1778, and GW to Sullivan, 28 Aug. 1778, *PGWRW* 16:401-2, 406-7
27. GW to Nathanael Greene, September 1, 1778, in *PGWRW*, 16:458-59.
28. GW to Nathanael Greene, September 1, 1778, in *PGWRW*, 16:458-59.
29. GW to Lafayette, September 1, 1778, *PGWRW*, 16:460-461.
30. GW to d'Estaing, 2 Sept. 1778, *PGWRW* 16:468-70; d'Estaing to GW, 5 Sept. 1778, *PGWRW* 16:522-25; d'Estaing to GW, 17 Sept. 1778, *PGWRW* 17:33-37.
31. Lafayette to GW, September 1, 1778, *PGWRW*, 16:461-64.
32. D'Estaing to GW, September 5, 1778, *PGWRW*, 16:522-25, quote on 524.
33. D'Estaing to GW, September 8, 1778, *PGWRW*, 16:540-42, quote on 541.
34. GW to D'Estaing, September 11-12, 1778, *PGWRW*, 16:570-74.
35. GW to Charles Scott, September 25, 1778, *PGWRW*, 17:132-134, quote on 132. In his book about the Culper spy ring, *Washington's Spies: The Story of America's First Spy Ring* (New York: Bantam Books, 2006), Alexander Rose fails to discuss the alliance as the reason for the creation of the Culper spy network; see page 78.
36. Benjamin Tallmadge to Charles Scott, October 29, 1778, in n.3 to Charles Scott to GW, October 29, 1778, in *PGWRW* 17:635-37.
37. See Jean Holker to GW, November 6, 1778, *PGWRW*, 18:56-57.
38. GW to Benjamin Tallmadge, November 29, 1778, *PGWRW*, 18:341.
39.GW to d'Estaing, September 11-12, 1778, *PGWRW*, 16:570-574.
40. Piers Mackesy, *The War for America 1775-1783* (1964. Reprint, Lincoln, NE, 1993), 254.
41. GW to Benjamin Harrison, October 25, 1779, *PGWRW*, 23:33-35.
42. GW to Maj. Gen. Lafayette, December 29, 1778, *PGWRW*, 18:526-27.
43. GW to the Continental Congress Committee of Conference, January 8, 1779, *PGWRW*, 18:594.
44. GW's memorandum to the Continental Congress Committee of Conference, January 8, 1778, enclosed in his letter to the committee of that date, *PGWRW*, 18:594-597.
45. Duane to GW, January 9, 1779, *PGWRW*, 18:605.

46. GW to James Duane, January 11-12, 1779, *PGWRW*, 18:612-15.

47. GW to the Continental Congress Committee of Conference, January, 13, 1779, *PGWRW*, 18:624-31; and GW to Philip Schuyler, January 18, 1779, *PGWRW*, 19:18-19; see also GW to James Duane, January, 11-12, 1779, *PGWRW*, 18:612-15.

48. On January 20, he submitted a paper on officers' pay; on January 23, he presented a paper on clothing the army; on January 23-31 he gave the committee a paper on artillery corps organization, the commissariat, barrack masters, and appointment of brigadiers; and on February 2 a paper on the ordnance department; *PGWRW*, 19:38-43, 52-62, 122-23.

49. JCC, 13:109-110.

50. James Duane, John Jay, William Floyd, and Francis Lewis to George Clinton, February 19, 1779, *PGWRW*, 19:356.

51. James Duane to Philip Schuyler, February 20, 1779, *PGWRW*, 19:218.

CHAPTER TWO: PROVISIONS, CLOTHES, MEN, VIRTUE, AND NATION

1. GW to John Jay, January 30, 1779, *PGWRW*, 23:108-9.

2. GW to Maj. Gen. Alexander McDougall, February 9, 1779, *PGWRW*, 23:156-61.

3. Circular to the States, August 28, 1779, PGWRW, 22:276-77.

4. GW to Samuel Huntington, December 10-11, 1779, *PGWRW*, 23:567-70.

5. GW to Samuel Huntington, December 13, 1779; Royal Flint to GW, December 12, 1779; and Henry Champion to Jeremiah Wadsworth, December 3, 1779, in *PGWRW*, 23:598-600.

6. Royal Flint to GW's aide-de-camp Lt. Col. Alexander Hamilton, December 23, 1779, *PGWRW*, 23:599-600.

7. GW to Samuel Huntington, December 15, 1779, *PGWRW*, 23:622-23.

8. Circular to the States, December 16, 1779, *PGWRW*, 23:627-29.

9. William Livingston to GW, December 19, 1779, *PGWRW*, 23:652-55.

10. Joseph Reed to GW, December 22, 1779, *PGWRW*, 23:687-89.

11. George Clinton to GW, December 26, 1779, *PGWRW*, 23:726-29.

12. Thomas Sim Lee to GW, December 26, 1779, *PGWRW*, 23:735-37.

13. These certificates were accepted as payment for state taxes, and the Continental Congress accepted them as payment for requisitions it made on the states. After the war, the remaining, unredeemed certificates were merged in the mass of federal debt. See E. James Ferguson, *The Power of the Purse* (Chapel Hill: University of North Carolina Press, 1961), 57-69.

14. Circular to the New Jersey Magistrates, January 7, 1780, *PGWRW*, 24:49-52.

15. GW to Lt. Col. William De Hart (and other officers), January 8, 1780, *PGWRW*, 24:57-60.

16. GW's memorandum to the Continental Congress Committee of Conference, January 8, 1779, *PGWRW*, 18:596.

17. GW to Continental Congress Committee of Conference, January 23, 1779, *PGWRW*, 19:52-57.

18. GW to John Jay, March 15, 1779, *PGWRW*, 19:486-89.
19. GW to James Wilkinson, December 19, 1779, *PGWRW*, 23:655.
20. GW to Nathanael Greene, December 20, 1779, *PGWRW*, 23:658-59.
21. Memorandum to the Continental Congress Committee of Conference, January 8, 1779, and GW to the Continental Congress Committee of Conference, January 13, 1779, *PGWRW*, 18:594, 624-31.
22. GW to John Jay, March 15, 1779, in John C. Fitzpatrick, ed., *The Writings of George Washington from the Original Manuscript Sources 1745-1799*, 39 vols. (Washington, DC: United States Government Printing Office, 1931-1944), 14:241-45.
23. GW to Gouverneur Morris, May 8, 1779, *PGWRW*, 20:384-86.
24. The expedition against the Iroquois; see chapter 3.
25. Circular to the States, May 22, 1779, *PGWRW*, 20:568-70.
26. GW to Maj. Gen. Benjamin Lincoln, July 30, 1779, *PGWRW*, 21:747-49.
27. GW to Joseph Reed, August 22, 1779, *PGWRW*, 22:224-27.
28. GW to Benjamin Harrison, December 18, 1778, in John Rhodehamel, ed., *George Washington: Writings* (New York: Library of America, 1997), 330-34.
29. GW to Benjamin Harrison, May 5-7, 1779, in Fitzpatrick, 15:5-11.
30. GW to George Mason, March 27, 1779, in Rhodehamel, 338-41.
31. GW to James Warren, March 31, 1779, in Rhodehamel, 341-43.
32. GW to William Fitzhugh, April 10, 1779, *PGWRW*, 20:30-32.
33. GW to Burwell Bassett, April 22, 1779, *PGWRW*, 20:160-61.
34. John Jay to GW, April 21, 1779, *PGWRW*, 20:150-51.
35. GW to John Jay, May 10, 1779, *PGWRW*, 20:421-22.
36. GW to John Armstrong, May 18, 1779, in Fitzpatrick, 15:96-99.
37. GW to Lund Washington, May 29, 1779, in Fitzpatrick, 15: 180-81.
38. GW to Bryan Fairfax, June 30, 1779, *PGWRW*, 21:301-2.
39. GW to Edmund Randolph, August 1, 1779, *PGWRW*, 22:6-7.
40. GW to Jean Holker, August 17, 1779, in Fitzpatrick, 16:123.
41. GW to John Sullivan, August 24, 1779, in Fitzpatrick, 16:160-61.
42. GW to John Jay, September 7, 1779, in Fitzpatrick, 16:246-49.
43. GW to Benjamin Lincoln, September 28, 1779, in Fitzpatrick, 16:350-53.
44. GW to Lafayette, September 30, 1779, in Fitzpatrick, 16:368-76, quote 372-73.
45. GW to Edmund Pendleton, November 1, 1779, in Fitzpatrick, 17:51-53.
46. GW to Samuel Huntington, November 18, 1779, in Fitzpatrick, 17:125-33.
47. GW to the Board of War, August 21, 1779, *PGWRW*, 22:196.
48. GW to Lund Washington, May 19, 1780, Rosenbach Museum and Library, Philadelphia, PA.

CHAPTER THREE: SUMMER 1779

1. James Thacher, *Military Journal of the American Revolution* (Hartford, CT: Hurlbut, Williams, & Company, 1862), 162.
2. Thacher, 162-63.
3. By "dependencies" GW meant the outlying posts in the New York City area, such as Paulus Hook, NJ, Staten Island, Brooklyn, and King's Bridge.

4. GW to Conrad-Alexandre Gérard, May 1, 1779; and GW to Gouverneur Morris, May 8, 1779, *PGWRW*, 20:279-81, 384-86.
5. Gérard to GW, May 5, 1779, *PGWRW*, 20:331-32.
6. GW to Gérard, May 18, 1779, *PGWRW*, 20:526-27.
7. Gérard's letter to Congress of May 9 and his memorandum of the same date to Congress are printed in *PGWRW*, 20:426-27.
8. JCC, 14:568.
9. Jay to GW, May 10, 1779, PGWRW 20:425-26.
10. See chapter 1.
11. GW to John Augustine Washington, May 12, 1779, *PGWRW*, 20:459-63.
12. GW to James Duane, January 11-12, 1779, *PGWRW*, 18:612-14.
13. See, for instance, GW to Philip Schuyler, February 11 and March 25, 1779; Schuyler to GW, March 1-7, 1779; Brig. Gen. Edward Hand to GW, March 29 and 31, 1779; and Questions and Answers Regarding a Proposed Expedition Against the Six Nations, March-April 1779, *PGWRW*, 19:176-79, 307-15, 676-89, 646-48, 667-68. See also Maj. Gen. John Sullivan to GW, April 16, 1779; GW to George Clinton, April 17 and May 3 and 24,1779; GW to Joseph Reed, April 19 and 27, 1779; GW to the Board of War, May 23 and 27, 1779; GW to Sullivan, May 8, 23-24, 24 (two letters), and 28, 1779; and GW to John Jay, 15 August 1779, *PGWRW*, 20:90-95, 105-6, 305-6, 596-97, 136-37, 237-42, 580-81, 642-43, 399, 589-91, 605-7, 666-67, and 22:124-30.
14. Washington first offered the command to Maj. Gen. Horatio Gates, who was senior to Sullivan, but Gates declined the command (see GW to Gates, March 6, 1779, and Gates to GW, March 16, 1779, in *PGWRW*, 19:377-78, 501-2.
15. GW to John Sullivan, May 31, 1779, first letter, *PGWRW*, 20:716-19.
16. For Sullivan's reports to GW during and immediately following the expedition, see Sullivan to GW, August 30 and September 28, 1779, *PGWRW*, 22:301-4, 528-41. For an excellent account of the Sullivan expedition and the Battle of Newtown, see Glenn F. Williams, *Year of the Hangman: George Washington's Campaign Against the Iroquois* (Yardley, PA: Westholme Publishing, 2005), 240-96.
17. "Address from the Delaware Nation," May 10, 1779, in *PGWRW*, 20: 414-17.
18. "Address to the Delaware Nation," May 12, 1779, *PGWRW*, 20:447-49.
19. Thacher, 163.
20. GW to John Jay, May 14, 1779, *PGWRW*, 20:490.
21. GW to Daniel Brodhead, May 21, 1779, *PGWRW*, 20:551-52; Brodhead convened the court-martial in June, but the court acquitted the soldier, see *PGWRW*, 20:553.
22. See Colin G. Calloway, *The American Revolution in Indian Country: Crisis and Diversity in Native America* (Cambridge: Cambridge University Press, 1995), 36-39, 171.
23. Mackesy, 252. For the formulation of the plan, see Mackesy, 254-56.
24. Germain to Clinton, January 23, 1779, in William B. Willcox, ed., *The American Rebellion: Sir Henry Clinton's Narrative of His Campaigns, 1775-*

1782, with an Appendix of Original Documents (New Haven: Yale University Press, 1954), 397-99; see also Mackesy, 255.

25. Mackesy, 254-56.

26. Mackesy, 269.

27. Mackesy, 269.

28. Willcox, 121-22.

29. Willcox, 121-23.

30. Willcox, 122-23.

31. Collier to Lord George Germain, May 22, and Mathew to Clinton, May 24 in K.G. Davies, ed., *Documents of the American Revolution, 1770-1783*; (Colonial Office Series), 21 vols. (Shannon and Dublin, Ireland, 1972-81), 17:130-34; Scott to GW, May 12, 18 and 27, 1779, *PGWRW*, 20:457, 530-31, 650-51; and Harry Miller Lydenberg, ed., *Archibald Robertson, Lieutenant-General Royal Engineers: His Diaries and Sketches in America, 1762-1780* (New York: New York Public Library, 1930), 193.

32. Willcox, 123.

33. GW to John Augustine Washington, June 20, *PGWRW*, 21:198.

34. GW to John Jay, May 25, 1779, *PGWRW*, 20:621.

35. GW to McDougall, May 28, and GW to Putnam, May 28, *PGWRW*, 20:600-602; for Washington's intelligence regarding the attack, see Elijah Hunter to GW, May 21, and Israel Shreve to GW, May 23, 1779, *PGWRW*, 20:556-57, 588-89.

36. GW to John Jay, June 6, 1779, *PGWRW*, 89-90; Lydenberg, 193-94; Christopher Ward, *The War of the Revolution*, 2 vols. (New York: Macmillan, 1952), 2:596-97; and Willcox, 125-26.

37. GW to John Jay, June 3, 1779, *PGWRW*, 21:36-37; GW to Maj. Gen. Alexander McDougall, May 31 and June 2, 1779, *PGWRW* 20:709-10, and 21:21; and GW to Maj. Gen. Stirling, June 3, *PGWRW*, 21:48-49..

38. GW to Brig. Gen. William Woodford, May 31, 1779, *PGWRW*, 20:723.

39. See William Malcom to GW and GW to Malcom, both June 5, *PGWRW*, 21:79-81.

40. Willcox, 125-26.

41. Willcox, 126-29, and Davies, 17:146.

42. GW to John Jay, June 6, 1779, *PGWRW*, 21:89-90.

43. GW to John Jay, June 11, 1779, *PGWRW*, 21:133.

44. Washington to William Fitzhugh, June 25, 1779, *PGWRW*, 21:241-44.

45. GW to John Augustine Washington, June 20, 1779, *PGWRW*, 21:198-99.

46. Washington to William Fitzhugh, June 25, 1779, *PGWRW*, 21:241-44.

47. GW to John Augustine Washington, June 20, 1779, *PGWRW*, 21:198-99.

48. Circular to the General Officers, June 13, 1779, and the enclosed "Contingency Orders" of June 12, 1779, *PGWRW*, 21:154-56.

49. GW to Maj. Gen. Alexander McDougall, June 19, 1779, *PGWRW*, 21:188-89.

50. GW to John Jay, June 23, 1779, *PGWRW*, 21:218.

51. See GW to Maj. Gen. Arthur St. Clair, July 20, 1779, *PGWRW*, 21:588; and GW to Brig. Gen. Henry Knox, August 20, 1779, *PGWRW*, 22:188-90.

52. GW to Maj. Gen. Arthur St. Clair, July 20, 1779, *PGWRW*, 21:588.
53. See Council of General Officers, July 26,1779 (second council) and the responses of July 27, 1779, in *PGWRW*, 21: 667-69, 674-702.
54. Willcox, 129-30. GW, in addition to the brigades in the West Point garrison, kept four brigades and some cavalry east of the Hudson River.
55. Willcox, 130.
56. William Tryon to Clinton, July 20, 1779, in Davies, 17:162-65.
57. GW to Brig. Gen. John Glover, July 8, 1779, *PGWRW*, 21:383-84.
58. GW to John Jay, July 13, *PGWRW*, 21:466.
59. GW to Norwalk, Conn., Officials, July 11, 1779, *PGWRW*, 21:441.
60. Brig. Gen. Samuel Holden Parsons to GW, July 9, 1779, *PGWRW*, 21:406; see also Norwalk, Conn., Officials and Lieutenant Colonel Stephen St. John to GW, July 9, 1779, in *PGWRW*, 21:403-4.
61. GW to John Jay, July 9, 1779, *PGWRW*, 21:397. For reactions of outrage in Congress, see James Lovell to Benjamin Lincoln, July 16; Henry Laurens to John Laurens, July 17; and Thomas McKean to Sarah McKean, July 20, in Paul H. Smith et al., eds., *Letters of Delegates to Congress, 1774-1789*. 26 vols. (Washington, DC: Library of Congress, 1976-2000), 13:236, 249-50, 237.
62. William Tryon to Henry Clinton, July 20, 1779, in Davies, 17:165.
63. GW to John Jay, July 13, 1779, *PGWRW*, 21:466.
64. Willcox, 131.
65. GW to John Jay, July 13, 1779, *PGWRW*, 21:466.
66. GW to Brig. Gen. Anthony Wayne, July 1, 1779, *PGWRW*, 21:326-27.
67. GW to Brig. Gen. Anthony Wayne, July 9,1779, *PGWRW*, 21:410-11.
68. Ward, 2:597. Ward writes "the grenadier company of the 71st," but the regiment was unusual in having two grenadier companies. Maj. Gen. James Pattison says that "two Companies of the 71st (Grenadiers)" were part of the garrison [James Pattison], "Official Letters of Major General James Pattison," in *Collections of the New-York Historical Society for the Year 1875*, 8 (1876; 1-430), 96.
69. GW to John Jay, July 21, 1779, *PGWRW*, 21:597.
70. Brig. Gen. Anthony Wayne to GW, July 3, 1779, *PGWRW*, 21:341-42.
71. GW to John Jay, July 21, 1779, *PGWRW*, 21:596-600.
72. GW to John Jay, July 21, 1779, *PGWRW*, 21:596-600.
73. GW to Brig. Gen. Anthony Wayne, July 10, 1779, *PGWRW*, 21:432-34.
74. Wayne to GW, July 15, 1779, *PGWRW*, 21:508.
75. "Plan of Attack," July 15, 1779, *PGWRW*, 21:509-10.
76. Wayne to GW, July 16, 1779 (second letter), *PGWRW*, 21:523-24.
77. See Ward, 1:358-59.
78. This quote and those in the preceding two paragraphs are taken from Wayne to GW, July 17, 1779, PGWRW, 21:541-43; see also Ward, 2:596-603; and Christopher L. Ward, *The Delaware Continentals 1776-1783* (Wilmington: Historical Society of Delaware, 1941), 291-302.
79. Wayne to GW, July 16, 1779 (second letter), *PGWRW*, 21:523-24.
80. GW to John Jay, July 21, 1779, and GW to Maj. Gen. Robert Howe, July 17, 1779, *PGWRW*, 21:560-600, 529-30.

81. Willcox, 132.
82. Willcox, 132.
83. Willcox, 133.
84. GW to John Jay, July 21, 1779, *PGWRW*, 21:596-600.
85. GW to Maj. Gen. Israel Putnam July 20, 1779, *PGWRW*, 21:586-87.
86. The council of war was held on July 26. Many, Maj. Gen. Arthur St. Clair in particular, pointed out the strategic importance of the posts to any British offensive against West Point. Several recommended moving corps of the army south on both sides of the river but only to threaten the outposts. Among those recommending attacking the King's Ferry outposts, most proposed attacking Stony Point, as that post militarily dominated Verplanck Point (the notable exceptions were brigadier generals Nixon and Parsons who thought GW should attack both posts simultaneously). St. Clair thought, "the greatest advantages would flow" from an attack on Stony Point. Kalb proposed that GW move a corps down to harass Stony Point, "strike a blow" against it if possible, and defend the supply route through Smith's Clove, NY. (see Council of War, July 26, and the generals' responses of July 27, 1779, *PGWRW*, 21:667-69, 674-702).
87. GW to Maj. Gen. Robert Howe, August 9, 1779, *PGWRW*, 22:71-73.
88. Description and map based on sketch in Johann Ewald, *Diary of the American War: A Hessian Journal*. Translated and edited by Joseph P. Tustin (New Haven: Yale University Press, 1979), 176-177, which shows the post at the time of the attack. The map in the Clements library, which appears in Freeman, 5, and is the basis for map in Ward, *Delaware Continentals*, shows the post as it appeared a year earlier in July 1778.
89. Pattison, "Letters," 99-100.
90. Pattison, "Letters," 100. The Royal Garrison Battalion was a provisional corps made up of British regular troops no longer fit for the long marches and rough conditions of campaigning with their regiments but still able to serve in a garrison.
91. See GW to Henry Lee, August 10, 1779, and n.1, and GW to Stirling, August 12; see also GW to Henry Lee, September 1, 1779; all citations of GW correspondence here and following are to *PGWRW*, 22, unless otherwise noted.
92. GW to John Jay, August 23, 1779 (second letter).
93. Richard Kidder Meade to Lee, July 28, 1779. Lee's letter has not been found.
94. GW to Maj. Henry Lee, September 1, 1779.
95. Capt. Allan McLane, commanding the infantry of Lee's corps, recorded in his journal on July 31 that he shifted the infantry and that night took post near Liberty Pole, NJ (NHi: McLane Papers). McLane's entries from August 1 to 16 detail the activities of his patrols in this area.
96. GW to Lee, August 10, and September 1; Lee's letter of August 11 submitting the plan has been lost; GW to Lee, August 12, and GW to Stirling, same date (first letter); Lee to Allen McLane, August 14, McLane's letter book, NHi: McLane Papers.
97. GW to Lee and GW to Stirling, both August 12.
98. Lee to GW, August 22, 1779; and Lee's statements in his Order of March.
99. Lee to Allen McLane, August 1, 1779, NHi: McLane Papers.

100. McLane's journal, NHi: McLane Papers.

101. Lee's "Order of march and disposition of battle," which he enclosed with his August 22 report to GW.

102. Unless otherwise noted, all details of the march, attack, and retreat, and quotes of Maj. Henry Lee are taken from his report to GW of August 22, and Lee's "Order of march and disposition of battle," which he enclosed with his report. *PGWRW*, 22:210-22.

103. Ward, *Delaware Continentals*, 306.

104. Maj. Henry Lee to Joseph Reed, August 27, 1779, in William B. Reed, *Life and Correspondence of Joseph Reed*, vol. 2 (Philadelphia, 1847), 126-27.

105. Ward, *Delaware Continentals*, 307.

106. Pattison, "Letters," 100-101; Carl Leopold Baurmeister, *Revolution in America: Confidential Letters and Journals, 1776-1784, of Adjutant General Major Baurmeister of the Hessian Forces.* Translated and annotated by Bernhard A. Uhlendorf (New Brunswick, NJ: Rutgers University Press, 1957), 295; and Ewald, 175. Pattison says the Hessians were from Regiment von Knyphausen, but von Schaller was a captain in Regiment Erbprinz and Ewald and Baurmeister make reference to Hessians from this regiment being assigned to Paulus Hook.

107. Sir Henry Clinton to Lord George Germain, August 21, 1779, in Davies, 17: 190. See also Baurmeister, 295.

108. Baurmeister, 295. Ewald, 175. Baurmeister says they were asleep; Ewald reports their composition only and says nothing about them being asleep but says the invalids in one of the blockhouses were asleep.

109. Pattison, "Letters," 100.

110. Pattison, "Letters," 100.

111. Pattison, "Letters," 101.

112. Carson I. A. Ritchie, ed., "A New York Diary of the Revolutionary War." *New-York Historical Society Quarterly* 50 (1966), 433.

113. Pattison, "Letters," 100. Baurmeister, 295. Henry Clinton reported that Sutherland took post in the redoubt with forty Hessians. Sir Henry Clinton to Lord George Germain, August 21, 1779, in Davies, 17:191.

114. Baurmesiter, 296. Ewald wrote on Schaller's defense of the redoubt: "He was scarcely in it when the Americans shouted to him that he was completely surrounded: he must surrender or he would receive no quarter. The captain replied that if they wanted to have him they should attack him, for they both would have more honor from the affair. He then fired and defended his post until daybreak, whereupon the Americans withdrew." Ewald, 175.

115. Pattison, "Letters," 101.

116. Ward, *Delaware Continentals*, 309.

117. British Maj. Gen. John Pattison later expressed amazement at this lack of destruction: "What is nearly as Extraordinary as the Enterprize itself & the Success of it, is that the Enemy, tho' in full Possession of the Fort, did not Spike up a Gun, destroy the Ammunition or do the least Injury to any of the Buildings." Pattison, "Letters," 101.

118. Sir Henry Clinton to Lord George Germain, August 21, 1779, in Davies, 17:191.

119. Lee's undated "Return of Prisoners taken at Powles Hook on the Morning of the 19th of August 1779," signed by Capt. Robert Forsyth by order of Lee, lists the numbers of prisoners captured by rank and includes their regiments. For the infantry captured, it lists one captain, four subalterns, one surgeon, one surgeon's mate, one quartermaster, nine sergeants, and 128 rank and file. For the artillery captured, the return lists one sergeant, one corporal, two gunners, and nine matrosses. In sum, it reports 158 total prisoners taken, including the ten "Inhabitants" who were counted in the infantry total. A note reads: "The surgeon on parole" (National Archives, Papers of the Continental Congress, item 152). The British sources give conflicting numbers for the prisoners taken. Maj. Gen. Pattison, commanding the New York garrison, reported four officers, seven sergeants, five corporals, and ninety-seven privates "taken or missing" (Pattison, "Letters," 101). A contemporary journal—probably kept either by Pattison or an officer on his staff—mentions "about 150" of the garrison captured (Ritchie, "New York Diary," 433), which accords with Lee's report of prisoners taken. Baurmeister, 296, claimed that many of the prisoners were "intoxicated."

120. The American casualty figures are from Howard H. Peckham, *The Toll of Independence: Engagements & Battle Casualties of the American Revolution* (Chicago: University of Chicago Press, 1974), 63-64. They are close to Lee's estimate at the time (in his report to GW) that his total of killed, wounded, and missing did not exceed twenty. The British figures are from Pattison's report (Pattison, "Letters," 101). Pattison did not list any officers as killed during the assault. Lee reported to Washington at the time that he had killed "not more than fifty of the Enemy" and wounded a few. Pattison claimed that in the whole of the fighting, including the skirmish at the Liberty Pole, the British captured eleven Americans (Pattison, "Letters," 101).

121. Ritchie, "New York Diary," 433.

122. Pattison, "Letters," 101; Baurmeister, *Revolution in America*, 296; and Ritchie, "New York Diary," 433-34.

123. Probably meaning the Bergen road.

124. On the bridge and removal of the planks: Samuel Shaw to Mr. Eliot, 30 Sept. 1779, in *Life and Journals of Major Samuel Shaw* (Boston, 1847), 64-70.

125. Peckham, *Toll of Independence*, 63-64. Pattison claimed that Buskirk captured four prisoners (Pattison, *Letters*, 101). Clinton also stated that Buskirk captured four men (Clinton to Germain, August 21, in Davies, 17:191).

126. Pattison, *Letters*, 101; Ritchie, "New York Diary," 434. Pattison claimed that the Guard's light infantry with Sutherland captured a captain and six prisoners on their march, which implies that Sutherland caught up with at least the stragglers from Lee's columns (Pattison, *Letters*, 101). Clinton stated that Sutherland made contact with Lee's rear-guard (Clinton to Germain, August 21, 1779, in Davies, 17:191). Ritchie, "New York Diary," says that these prisoners were stragglers (434).

127. Ritchie, "New York Diary," 434.

128. Lee to GW, August 22, 1779, *PGWRW*, 22:210-17.

129. GW to Stirling, August 21; GW to Henry Lee, August 22; Lee to GW, 22 Aug.; and GW to Lee, 23 August 23, 1779.

130. Greene to Catharine Greene, August 23, 1779, in Richard K. Showman et al., eds. *The Papers of General Nathanael Greene*, 13 vols. (Chapel Hill: University of North Carolina Press, 1976-2005), 4:333-34; Greene to George Weedon, 6 September 1779, in Showman, 4:364-65.

131. Alexander Hamilton to John Laurens, September 11, 1779, in Harold C. Syrett et al., eds., *The Papers of Alexander Hamilton*, 27 vols. (New York: Columbia University Press, 1961-87), 2:168; Samuel Shaw to Mr. Eliot, 30 Sept. 1779, in *Life and Journals of Major Samuel Shaw*, 64-70; Pattison, "Letters," 99.

132. GW to Lee, August 23, 1779, *PGWRW*, 22:231-32.

133. GW to John Jay, August 23, 1779 (second letter). The report included Lee's order of march and his return of prisoners.

134. Henry Lee to GW, August 22, 1779, and GW to Stirling, August 21, 1779, *PGWRW*, 22: 210-17, 206; Davies, 17:190-91; and Willcox, 139-40; see also William B. Willcox, *Portrait of a General: Sir Henry Clinton in the War of Independence* (New York: Alfred A. Knopf, 1964), 279.

135. See GW to Maj. Gen. Robert Howe, August 18, 1779, *PGWRW*, 22:171-72.

136. Substance of a Conference with La Luzerne, September 16, 1779, *PGWRW*, 22:438-42.

137. GW to Maj. Gen. Lafayette, September 30, 1779, *PGWRW*, 22:559.

CHAPTER FOUR: ATTACK ON NEW YORK

1. Willcox, *American Rebellion*, 127.

2. Davies, 17:116, 124.

3. Willcox, *American Rebellion*, 140; see also Lydenberg, 202.

4. Willcox, *American Rebellion*, 141.

5. Willcox, *American Rebellion*, 126, 140; Lydenberg, 202.

6. See chapter 3 and GW to William Livingston, May 4, 1779; GW to Benjamin Harrison, May 5-7, and GW to John Jay, May 5, *PGWRW* 20:321-23, 332-36, 337-38.

7. Board of General Officers to GW, July 22, 1779, *PGWRW*, 21:612-14.

8. GW to Maj. Gen. Robert Howe, June 25, 1779, *PGWRW*, 21:250-51.

9. Thoughts on Defense of West Point, July 1779, *PGWRW*, 21:772-73.

10. GW to Maj. Gen. Robert Howe, September 7, 1779 (all references to GW's correspondence here and following are to *PGWRW*, 22, unless otherwise noted).

11. GW to Col. David Hall and to Col. Moses Hazen, both August 28.

12. GW to Maj. Gen. Robert Howe, August 28; see also GW to Howe, September 5.

13. GW to Maj. Gen. Stirling, August 28-29.

14. GW to Maj. Gen. Robert Howe, GW to Maj. Benjamin Tallmadge, and GW to Lt. Col. John Taylor, all August 28.

15. GW to Maj. Gen. William Heath, August 29.

16. GW to the Officer Commanding Major Lee's Corps, August 29.

17. GW to John Jay, September 7 (second letter).

18. GW to Maj. Gen. Robert Howe, September 7 and 18.

19. For these reports, see Maj. Gen. Horatio Gates to GW, September 6, 1779; Brig. Gen. Jedediah Huntington to GW, September 11, 1779; GW to Huntington, September 12, 1779; GW to Gates and Brig. Gen. Anthony Wayne, both September 14, 1779; and GW to John Jay, September 19-20, 1779.

20. See GW to John Jay, September 25.

21. Some planning had already begun for such attacks in late July. See Council of General Officers, 26 July (second council) and the responses of Maj. Gen. Nathanael Greene, Maj. Gen. Alexander McDougall, and Maj. Gen. Arthur St. Clair, all dated July 27, PGWRW, 21:667-68, 674-702; see also GW to Brig. Gen. Henry Knox, August 20.

22. These numbers are totals of rank and file fit for duty on the army's October 1779 returns, not including artillery; see Charles H. Lesser, ed., *The Sinews of Independence: Monthly Strength Reports of the Continental Army* (Chicago: University of Chicago Press, 1976), 136-39. The army's strength including officers and noncommissioned officers was over twenty thousand, not including artillery.

23. GW to Maj. Gen. Horatio Gates, September 14.

24. GW to Vice Admiral d'Estaing, September 13, 1779.

25. GW to Maj. Gen. Stirling, September 14, 1779; GW issued no direct orders to Wayne, but the light infantry corps was already stationed in the vicinity of Stony Point.

26. GW to Maj. Gen. Robert Howe, September 13, 1779.

27. GW to Vice Admiral d'Estaing, September 13, 1779.

28. See Willcox, *American Rebellion*, 145, n.1.

29. Brig. Gen. Henry Knox to GW, July 27, 1779. Knox was replying to GW's request for opinions regarding strategy posed at a council of war on July 26.

30. Brig. Gen. Henry Knox to GW, September 30, 1779; see also GW to Maj. Gen. William Heath, September 29, 1779 (second letter).

31. John Jay to GW, September 26, 1779.

32. Jay to GW, September 26, 1779; Journals of the Continental Congress (hereafter JCC), 15:1108.

33. Jay's letter to GW was dated September 26, 1779. GW replied to Samuel Huntington, the new president of Congress: "Sir: I had the honor of receiving your Excellency's letter of the 26th and 27th ultimo at half after twelve O'Clock yesterday. I immediately upon the Receipt of it, I set about concerting the measures necessary for cooperation with His Excellency the Count D'Estaing, agreeable to the powers vested in me by the Resolve of Congress of the 26th ulto." (GW to Huntington, October 4, 1779).

34. Stirling's plan dealt with an attack on Staten Island; St. Clair's plan dealt with attacks on Manhattan and Long Islands; see Maj. Gen. Arthur St. Clair to GW, October 4, and Stirling to GW, October 5, 1779. The previous proposals, submitted on July 27 in response to a query from GW to his generals, dealt with the prospects for attacks on the forts at King's Ferry. Brig. Gen. Anthony Wayne was one of the few to submit an actual plan of attack; see Wayne to GW, July 27, 1779, *PGWRW*, 21:701-2.

35. GW to Maj. Gen. Arthur St. Clair, October 4, 1779.

36. Since the Battle of Monmouth, many of GW's most trusted advisors and aggressive generals had urged him to take this course. GW's aide-de-camp Alexander Hamilton had labeled the council of war before Monmouth that had balked at attacking the British a "society of midwives"; see Hamilton to Elias Boudinot, 5 July 1778, in Syrett, 1:510. Brig. Gen. Anthony Wayne, Maj. Gen. Lafayette, and Maj. Gen. Nathanael Greene had each written a letter to GW urging him to overrule the council (all dated June 24, 1778, PGWRW, 15:525-26, 528-29, 534-35). GW accepted their arguments, overruled the council, and attacked. He fought the British to a draw in a battle that proved the mettle of his new army.

37. GW to James Mercer, October 14, 1779.

38. GW to George Clinton, October 1, 1779.

39. GW to Vice Admiral d'Estaing, September 13, 1779.

40. GW to George Clinton, October 4, 1779

41. GW to Vice Admiral d'Estaing, October 4, 1779; see also GW to d'Estaing, October 7, 1779 and GW to Brigadier General Duportail and Lt. Col. Alexander Hamilton, October 18, 1779.

42. If d'Estaing arrived before the militia assembled and supplies were ready for the New York campaign, d'Estaing could land his troops on Rhode Island and cooperate with Maj. Gen. Gates's two thousand troops in attacking Newport. Washington would send a division from the main army (proposed in GW to d'Estaing, October 4, 1779). (Washington asked Gates to provide him with information to determine the practicability of Gates and d'Estaing taking Newport while preparations for the attack on New York were completing [GW to Gates, October 3].)

43. GW to d'Estaing, October 4, 1779.

44. GW to d'Estaing, October 7, 1779, and GW to George Clinton, October 4, 1779. In case of a campaign against Newport/Rhode Island he expected to send only a lightly equipped division from the main army to reinforce Gates's and d'Estaing's troops (see GW to Greene, September 26). He directed Gates to plan and prepare for potential operations at Rhode Island (GW to Gates, September 14, and October 3; GW to Samuel Huntington, October 4). Though his letter to Huntington of October 4 makes it clear that GW realized d'Estaing might choose a campaign only against Newport, he did not mention a Newport-only campaign in his letter to d'Estaing of October 4.

45. GW to Brig. Gen. Duportail and Alexander Hamilton, October 21, 1779. Besides blocking the withdrawal or reinforcement of the outlying British garrisons by water GW wanted the fleet to ensure his army's retreat from Manhattan and Long Island if his attacks failed (see GW to Duportail and Hamilton, October 21). GW told Duportail and Hamilton on October 21 that the presence of the French fleet would be critical to securing the army's retreat from York and Long Island in case they found "that neither is practicable and we should be obliged to abandon the Enterprise." GW even wanted to augment the French admiral's strength. The commander in chief asked Congress to have the Continental frigates and other armed vessels to act in conjunction with d'Estaing's ships. In fact, the Marine Committee had already ordered the frigates to do just

that; see GW to Samuel Huntington, October 4 and GW to d'Estaing, same date, and John Matthews (of the Marine Committee) to GW, September 28; and GW to the Marine Committee, October 6, 1779.

46. GW to d'Estaing, October 4, 1779

47. D'Estaing's force consisted of twenty-two ships of the line, two fifties, and fourteen frigates. The British squadron at New York was composed of five ships of the line, two fifties, two forty-fours, and some smaller warships.

48. GW planned to have Maj. Henry Lee's Partisan Corps launch a surprise attack on the British fort at Sandy Hook, NJ, to aid the entry of the French fleet. Even after it was clear that the French fleet was not coming to New York, GW continued the plan in force (see GW to Lee, September 25, 1779; Lee to GW, December 16, 1779; and GW to Lee, December 20, 1779, the latter two letters in *PGWRW*, 23:632-33, 660). Capt. Henry Peyton of Lee's corps carried out the surprise assault on January 16 (see Lee to GW, January 17, *PGWRW*, 24:167-68).

49. Arbuthnot to Sir Peter Parker, October 20, 1779, in Davies, 17:234.

50. See Willcox, *American Rebellion*, 145 n 1.

51. GW to Edmund Pendleton, November 1, 1779, *PGWRW*, 23:121-22. For Arbuthnot's sinking of hulks, see his letter of October 30, 1779, to Lord Sandwich, in G. R. Barnes and J. H. Owen, eds., *The Private Papers of John, Earl of Sandwich, First Lord of the Admiralty, 1771-1782.* 4 vols., in *Publications of the Navy Records Society*, vols. 69, 71, 75, 78 (London: Scolar Press, 1932-38), 3:136-38. See also GW to Maj. Gen. Lafayette, October 20, 1779. For additional evidence that the measure was a failure, see Brig. Gen. Duportail and Lt. Col. Alexander Hamilton to GW, October 26, 1779, *PGWRW*, 23:51-54. This was probably the source for GW's remark to Pendleton. GW, though, realized the potential effectiveness of the British harbor defenses: "They work incessantly," he reported to Lafayette, "and will, it is feared, render the entrance into the Harbour extremely difficult, if not impracticable" if they could be completed before the French fleet arrived (GW to Lafayette, October 20, 1779).

52. GW to Vice Admiral d'Estaing, October 4, 1779.

53. GW to Vice Admiral d'Estaing, September 13, 1779.

54. GW's "Loose Thoughts upon an Attack of New York," October 3, 1779.

55. GW to Maj. Gen. Duportail and Lt. Col. Alexander Hamilton, October 18, 1779. GW proposed that Vice Admiral d'Estaing deploy "two or three fifty Gun Ships and as many Frigates" for this operation (GW to d'Estaing, October 4). GW had sent his French chief engineer, Duportail, and his French-speaking aide-de-camp Alexander Hamilton to meet the French fleet.

56. GW's "Loose thoughts upon an Attack of N. York," October 3, 1779. Unless otherwise noted, the elements of Washington's attack plan and the quotes are taken from this memorandum.

57. Many historians have taken at face value the claim of the French and American officers at the time of d'Estaing's attempted entry into the harbor in July 1778 that the French battle ships drew too much water to cross the bar. But Alfred Thayer Mahan gives evidence that casts doubt on these claims and argues

that the French fleet could have entered the harbor with knowledgeable pilots, northeast winds, and a spring tide; see Mahan, *The Major Operations of the Navies in the War of American Independence* (Little, Brown, and Company, 1913; reprint New York: Greenwood Press, 1969). GW clearly believed this to be the case as is seen from his strong efforts in obtaining the best pilots for the French ships. The British routinely passed sixty-four-gun ships over the bar.

58. GW to Maj. Henry Lee, October 10, 1779.

59. Vice Admiral d'Estaing's reluctance to attempt an entry into the harbor had prevented a combined campaign against New York in 1778. The allies instead opted for an attack on Newport, Rhode Island.

60. GW's Circular to Pilots, October 5, 1779; see also GW to the Marine Committee and Alexander Hamilton to the Marine Committee, both October 6.

61. GW to Thomas Hunt, October 5 and GW to the Marine Committee, October 7, 1779.

62. GW to Thomas Hunt, October 5, 1779; and GW to William Livingston, October 4, 1779.

63. See GW to Vice Admiral d'Estaing, October 4, 1779, and GW to John Mathews, October 10, 1779. GW arranged to have the family of the pilot, Abraham Marling, looked after. GW pointed out these obstructions to d'Estaing in his September 13, 1779 letter. Fearing that d'Estaing might bypass the Capes of Delaware where he had sent some of these pilots, the general personally rerouted one pilot to Monmouth Co., NJ, to "join the Count on the first appearance of the fleet" if the French admiral sailed directly for Sandy Hook; see GW to Maj. Henry Lee, October 10.

64. See GW to Major Generals Robert Howe and Stirling, both October 4, 1779.

65. GW to Brig. Gen. Anthony Wayne, October 10, 1779.

66. See GW to Major Generals Stirling and Robert Howe, both October 4, 1779, ordering them to execute his previous orders of September 13 and 14. The quotes are from GW's orders to Maj. Gen. Howe of September 13 and his orders to Maj. Gen. Stirling of September 14, 1779.

67. GW to Maj. Gen. Stirling, October 4, 1779; Stirling to GW, October 5, Brig. Gen. Anthony Wayne to GW, October 5, 1779, GW to Wayne, October 6, 1779, GW to Stirling, October 7, 1779, and GW to Brig. Gen. William Woodford, October 12, 1779.

68. GW to Brig. Gen. Anthony Wayne, October 10, 1779.

69. GW to Maj. Gen. Robert Howe, October 4 and 9, 1779.

70. See Lydenberg, 203 and [Stephen Kemble]. *The Kemble Papers*, 2 vols. (New York: New York Historical Society, 1884-85 in *Collections of the New-York Historical Society*, vols. 16–17), 1:186-87. On October 9, Clinton ordered the expeditionary troops held in readiness to embark; this order may have been a reaction to Brig. Gen. Antony Wayne's "grand forage" with the light infantry corps (see Wayne to GW, October 5).

71. GW to Vice Admiral d'Estaing, September 13, 1779.

72. GW to Brigadier General Duportail and Lieutenant Colonel Alexander Hamilton, October 10.

73. GW's "Loose Thoughts upon an Attack of New York," 3 October 1779.

74. GW to Maj. Gen. Robert Howe, September 13 and GW to Maj. Gen. Stirling, September 14, 1779; see also GW to Maj. Gen. William Heath, September 13, 1779, and GW to Heath, September 14, 1779; GW to Brig. Gen. Anthony Wayne, September 14, 1779; for the direct attacks on the forts at King's Ferry, see GW to Wayne, September 26, and October 3, 1779; GW to Heath, September 29, 1779 (second letter); Brig. Gen. Henry Knox to GW, September 30, 1779; and Wayne to GW, October 5, 1779.

75. GW to Maj. Gen. Stirling, September 29.

76. The surveys were to emphasize information on the ability of the fort to withstand a bombardment and to determine positions for artillery batteries.

77. Maj. Gen. Arthur St. Clair to GW, October 4, 1779. GW hoped to attack King's Ferry whether d'Estaing opted for an attack on New York or not. He wrote to Brig. Gen. Anthony Wayne on October 10: "A small time will determine whether these posts [Stony Point and Verplanck Point] or a greater object shall engage our attention." This part of the offensive plan looked back to the recommendations of St. Clair and Wayne in their July 27 council of war response: taking Stony Point by quick siege/bombardment and forcing the evacuation of Verplanck Point and the retreat of its garrison.

78. GW to Brig. Gen. Anthony Wayne, October 3, Wayne to GW, October 14, and Wayne to GW, October 9, 1779.

79. GW to Maj. Gen. William Heath, September 29.

80. See Maj. Gen. Stirling to GW, October 5, 1779, and its enclosure described in the docket of the letter as "Hints for attacking Staten Island."

81. In Stirling's proposed plan of attack (of October 5) Vice Admiral d'Estaing would make "a forcible push" to pass the Narrows with some of his ships and his troops would then land at Prince's Bay on the south side of the island and, after assembling boats for the crossing, the American troops would land on the north side of the island (Stirling listed specific embarkation points) near "Mercereau's Wharf." Stirling thought the capture of Staten Island the key to any combined operation against New York: Staten Island "we must carry." "When Staten Island is secured the other operations will be easy." GW's reply is dated October 7.

82. Quotes from GW to George Clinton, October 1; GW to Maj. Gen. Robert Howe, October 9, 1779; and GW to Vice Admiral d'Estaing, October 4; see also GW to d'Estaing, September 13, 1779; GW to Clinton, October 4, 1779; GW to Stirling, September 14, 1779.

83. GW to Vice Admiral d'Estaing, September 13, 1779.

84. GW to Vice Admiral d'Estaing, October 4, 1779.

85. GW to Maj. Gen. Stirling, September 14, 1779. On September 13, GW issued similar orders to Maj. Gen. Robert Howe.

86. GW to Maj. Gen. Howe, October 9, 1779.

87. GW to George Clinton, October 4, 1779.

88. See GW to Maj. Gen. Horatio Gates, October 3, 1779.

89. GW to Maj. Gen. Horatio Gates, October 3, 1779. Gates replied that he had anticipated the movement of his troops for the joint campaign and had assembled enough boats "to Transport Our whole Force, Artillery, Military Stores,

& Provisions at one Embarkation, to any place within a Boat Navigation," if the plan was to attack Rhode Island. He had prepared siege equipment. His troops were "ready to March at The Shortest Notice." If the plan was to use his troops in an attack on New York or Long Island, Gates reported that once the French fleet arrived he would "make a Landing with the Troops as High up the Sound as Morrisinia" or, if transports were not available, march his troops overland to New York. Gates further reported that Rhode Island would "readily consent" to taking their state troops with the Continentals, as Washington had requested (Gates to GW, October 8).

90. Maj. Gen. Arthur St. Clair to GW, October 4, 1779.

91. Maj. Gen. Arthur St. Clair to GW, October 4, 1779.

92. Maj. Gen. Arthur St. Clair to GW, October 4, 1779. Interestingly, St. Clair believed that a landing on Long Island involved "much less Risque than in forcing a Passage over Haarlem, or landing on York Island by the North River, as in either of these the Fate of America must, in a great Measure, be set upon a single Cast."

93. In another indication that GW planned for operations on Long Island, he told Brig. Gen. Duportail and Lt. Col. Alexander Hamilton on October 21 that the control of the Sound was critical to conducting operations on Long Island because his supplies during the operation would have to come across the Sound.

94. A large elevation north of the city's outer defenses, then located about three miles from the heart of the city. One road north from the city to King's Bridge crossed the hill and the other passed just to its west. GW appears to have planned to make this hill the center of his siege lines north of the city.

95. GW to Lt. Col. John Taylor or Maj. Samuel Hayes, October 10, 1779.

96. GW to Lt. Col. John Taylor, October 10, 1779.

97. GW to Maj. Henry Lee, October 7, 1779.

98. GW to Maj. Benjamin Tallmadge, October 6, 1779.

99. GW to Maj. Benjamin Tallmadge, October 8, 1779.

100. Report from Capt. James Monroe, October 9, 1779.

101. Willcox, *American Rebellion*, 141.

102. GW to Lt. Col. Alexander Hamilton and Brigadier General Duportail, October 10, 1779, and Report from Capt. James Monroe, October 9, 1779. GW considered it so important that the French admiral be met with "intelligence of the enemy's situation, and with good pilots to conduct him into the harbour," that he directed "at least half a dozen fast sailing boats" commanded by men "on whose fidelity we can absolutely rely" be kept constantly cruising off the New Jersey shore to deliver the pilots and his dispatches at the admiral's first appearance. GW to John Cox, October 4, 1779. Capt. James Monroe "late of the Armed Brig *Saratoga*," who had escaped from a prison ship in New York harbor, reported only three ships of the line, two heavy frigates (one dismasted), eight or ten frigates, and sloops of war at New York. He reported that they had added "twelve or fifteen" large unarmed vessels to these to form a line with the warships to make their numbers appear greater and that they were preparing to sink eleven ships at the Hook to narrow the passage into the harbor.

103. GW to Maj. Benjamin Tallmadge, October 9 and 14, 1779; see also GW to Tallmadge, October 6, 1779.

104. GW to Maj. Benjamin Tallmadge, October 14, 1779.

105. GW to Vice Admiral d'Estaing, October 4, 1779.

106. GW to George Clinton, October 4, 1779.

107. GW to Samuel Huntington, October 9, 1779.

108. Willcox, *American Rebellion*, 64.

109. GW to Maj. Gen. Lafayette, October 20, 1779.

110. See the reports of the Culper ring spy Robert Townsend in the notes of GW to Maj. Benjamin Tallmadge, October 2, 1779, GW to Samuel Huntington, October 9, 1779, and "Instructions to Major Benjamin Tallmadge," October 17, 1779.

111. GW to Brigadier General Duportail and Lt. Col. Alexander Hamilton, October 21, 1779.

112. GW to George Clinton, September 27, 1779.

113. GW to Col. Thomas Clark, GW to Col. Moses Hazen, and GW to Maj. Gen. John Sullivan, all October 3, 1779.

114. GW to George Clinton, October 4, 1779. See also, GW to Jonathan Trumbull, Sr., October 10, 1779, and GW to Clinton, September 27. GW had expectation that he could get ten thousand of these militiamen for the campaign: he ordered Greene to get tents sufficient for that number (see GW to Maj. Gen. Nathanael Greene, October 6). Properly equipped and organized militia from the states was "essential" to the campaign (see GW to Clinton, September 27). GW stipulated that the three months were to be from the time the militiamen joined the main army, not from the time they mustered.

115. GW to Maj. Gen. Nathanael Greene, September 26, 1779, and Greene to GW, September 27, 1779.

116. GW to Maj. Gen. Nathanael Greene, September 26, 1779.

117. GW to Maj. Gen. Nathanael Greene, October 6, 1779. Greene, GW wrote, was making "every possible preparation for Camp equipage," but expected to fall short in tents (GW to George Clinton, October 10). GW asked Massachusetts for the loan of 1,500 tents, the deficiency identified in the Continental stores (GW to Jeremiah Powell, October 7).

118. GW to Lt. Col. Mathew Mead, October 12 and 13. GW directed the letter to Mead, commander of one of the regiments, but GW asked Mead to communicate his request to the other commanders.

119. GW to James Wilkinson, October 5, 1779. Much has been made of the Continental army's lack of shoes, and the army was indeed short of footwear. GW told the Board of War that "a considerable part of the army" was unfit for marching or fatigue duty due to lack of shoes (GW to the Board of War, October 2; see also GW to the Board of War, October 12, where he claimed that a third of the army lacked shoes) and he made shoes for his soldiers one of his foremost priorities in preparing for these operations (as he told the Board on October 12, "a matter of so important a nature"). He urgently requested the commissaries of hides to send in all the shoes they could obtain "that we may endeavour to

get the whole Army shod" (GW to George Starr, October 2). But the documents also show that an ample supply of over twelve thousand pairs of shoes could have been available to the army in late October and early November; see Board of War to GW, October 9, and GW to the Board of War, October 25, 1779, *PGWRW*, 23:29-30.

120. GW to Jeremiah Wadsworth, September 26, 1779.

121. GW to Wadsworth, October 9, 1779. Wadsworth thought the he would be able to obtain a "full supply" of rum but was not optimistic about his ability to supply additional quantities of ship bread beyond the supplies he had in hand (see Wadsworth to GW, October 11, 1779).

122. Jeremiah Wadsworth to GW, September 26, 1779, and Washington to George Clinton, October 10, 1779. GW advised Gov. Clinton that the army's supply of flour appeared "extremely limited and unpromising" (GW to Clinton, 27 September). Wadsworth feared a shortage of flour for the campaign, but he assured Washington that he could provide meat in "any quantity that may be required" (GW to Clinton, October 10, 1779).

123. GW to George Clinton, October 1, 1779.

124. GW to George Clinton, October 4, 1779.

125. GW to Jonathan Trumbull, Sr. and to Jeremiah Powell, both October 7, 1779.

126. GW to George Clinton, October 4, 1779.

127. George Clinton to GW, October 7, 1779.

128. See the notes of GW to George Clinton, October 4, 1779; Massachusetts Council to GW, October 12, 1779; Jonathan Trumbull, Sr. to GW, October 14, 1779. Although GW agreed that some of the Connecticut quota could remain in their defensive positions on the Connecticut coast (the British had recently raided southern Connecticut towns), he asked Gov. Trumbull that they be formed into proper regiments, completely officered, and "in every respect ready to march at a moments warning." GW emphasized to Trumbull, as he would have no doubt emphasized to all the governors, that a failure to have their quota ready to march to join the Continental army "at a critical Moment, might be fatal to the whole plan of operations." (GW to Trumbull, October 10, 1779).

129. William Livingston to GW, October 7, 1779.

130. Massachusetts Council to GW, October 16, 1779; Jonathan Trumbull, Sr. to GW, October 14, 1779.

131. William Livingston to GW, October 8, 1779, n.3.

132. George Clinton to GW, October 7, 1779, and Clinton to Jeremiah Wadsworth, October 15 quoted in Wadsworth to GW, October 11, 1779, n.2; see also GW to Clinton, October 10, 1779.

133. GW to Maj. Gen. Lafayette, October 20, 1779.

134. See the editorial note "Planning for an Allied Attack on New York, c.3-7 October 1779."

135. GW to Vice Admiral d'Estaing, October 7, 1779. As the quote indicates, GW was prepared to hazard a winter campaign to gain a decisive victory. The length of service for militia (three months after joining the army) shows that he was prepared to campaign into January (see GW to George Clinton, October 4,

1779). And he ordered woolen overalls, watch coats, and woolen mitts forwarded to Newburg (see GW to James Wilkinson, October 5, 1779).

136. GW to Gouverneur Morris, May 8, 1779, *PGWRW*, 20:384-86.

137. GW to the Continental Congress Committee of Conference, January 13, 1779, *PGWRW*, 18:624-29.

138. GW to the Continental Congress Committee of Conference, January 13, 1779, *PGWRW*, 18:624-29.

139. GW to Gouverneur Morris, May 8, 1779, *PGWRW*, 20:384-86.

140. GW to Joseph Reed, December 12, 1778, and GW to Benjamin Harrison, December 18-30, 1778, *PGWRW*, 18:396-98, 447-50.

141. See John Jay to GW, August 18, 1779, n.2.

142. GW to Maj. Gen. John Sullivan, October 3, 1779.

143. Maj. Gen. Horatio Gates to GW, October 8, 1779, and GW to Gates, October 16, 1779.

144. Quoted in Willcox, *Henry Clinton*, 157.

145. GW to John Parke Custis, November 10, 1779, *PGWRW*, 23:224-25.

146. GW to Maj. Gen. Lafayette, October 20, 1779.

147. GW to Edmund Pendleton, November 1, 1779, *PGWRW*, 23:121-22

148. GW to John Parke Custis, November 10, 1779, *PGWRW*, 23:224-25.

149. GW to Samuel Huntington, November 14, 1779, *PGWRW*, 23:275-77; and GW to Maj. Gen. William Heath, November 16, 1779, *PGWRW*, 23:299-300.

150. GW to Brigadier General Duportail and Lt. Col. Alexander Hamilton, October 18, 1779, emphasis added.

151. GW to Samuel Huntington, October 21, 1779.

152. See Maj. Gen. Horatio Gates to GW, October 13, 1779, n.2.

153. See Davies, 17:236-37 and Barnes and Owen, 3:136-38; see also Willcox, *American Rebellion*, 145-47. For the British evacuation of the forts at King's Ferry, NY, see GW to Brig. Gen. Anthony Wayne, October 21 (second letter) and Wayne to GW, October 21, 1779. For GW's refortification of King's Ferry, see GW to Maj. Gen. William Heath, November 16, 1779, PGWRW, 23:299-300.

154. GW to Brig. Gen. Anthony Wayne, November 17, 1779, *PGWRW*, 23:316.

155. GW to Maj. Gen. Benjamin Lincoln, December 12, 1779, *PGWRW*, 23:584.

156. GW to Col. Thomas Clark, November 19, 1779, GW to Samuel Huntington, November 29, 1779, and GW to Brig. Gen. William Woodford, December 13, 1779, *PGWRW*, 23:344-45, 482-84, 602-3.

157. GW to Samuel Huntington, November 24, 1779, *PGWRW*, 23:415-18.

158. GW to Benjamin Harrison, October 25, 1779, *PGWRW*, 23:33-35.

159. GW to Maj. Gen. Robert Howe, November 20, 1779, *PGWRW*, 23:373-75.

BIBLIOGRAPHY

ARCHIVAL SOURCES

Library of Congress, Journals of the Continental Congress.
National Archives, Papers of the Continental Congress.
New-York Historical Society, McLane Papers.
Rosenbach Museum and Library, Philadelphia, PA.

PUBLISHED PRIMARY SOURCES

Barnes, G. R., and J. H. Owen, eds. *The Private Papers of John, Earl of Sandwich, First Lord of the Admiralty, 1771-1782.* 4 vols., in *Publications of the Navy Records Society*, vols. 69, 71, 75, 78. London: Scolar Press, 1932-38.

Baurmeister, Carl Leopold. *Revolution in America: Confidential Letters and Journals, 1776-1784, of Adjutant General Major Baur meister of the Hessian Forces.* Translated and annotated by Bernhard A. Uhlendorf. New Brunswick, NJ: Rutgers University Press, 1957.

Crackel, Theodore J., and Edward Lengel, et al., eds. *The Papers of George Washington Revolutionary War Series.* 25 vols. to date. Charlottesville: University of Virginia Press, 1985.

Davies, K.G., ed. *Documents of the American Revolution, 1770-1783 (Colonial Office Series).* 21 vols. Shannon and Dublin: Irish University Press, 1972-81.

Ewald, Johann. *Diary of the American War: A Hessian Journal.* Translated and edited by Joseph P. Tustin. New Haven: Yale University Press, 1979.

Fitzpatrick, John C., ed. *The Writings of George Washington from the Original Manuscript Sources 1745-1799,* 39 vols. Washington, DC: United States Government Printing Office, 1931-1944.

Ford, Worthington Chauncey, et al., eds. *Journals of the Continental Congress, 1774-1789.* 34 vols. Washington, DC: Library of Congress, 1904-37.

[Kemble, Stephen]. *The Kemble Papers*. 2 vols. New York: New York Historical Society, 1884-85 in *Collections of the New-York Historical Society*, vols. 16–17.

Lesser, Charles H., ed. *The Sinews of Independence: Monthly Strength Reports of the Continental Army*. Chicago: University of Chicago Press, 1976.

Lydenberg, Harry Miller, ed. *Archibald Robertson, Lieutenant-General Royal Engineers: His Diaries and Sketches in America, 1762-1780*. New York: New York Public Library, 1930.

[Pattison, James], "Official Letters of Major General James Pattison," in *Collections of the New-York Historical Society for the Year 1875*. Vol. 8. 1876.

Peckham, Howard H. *The Toll of Independence: Engagements & Battle Casualties of the American Revolution*. Chicago: University of Chicago Press, 1974.

Reed, William B. *Life and Correspondence of Joseph Reed*. Vol. 2. Philadelphia, 1847.

Rhodehamel, John, ed. *George Washington: Writings*. New York: Library of America, 1997.

Ritchie, Carson I. A., ed. "A New York Diary of the Revolutionary War." *New-York Historical Society Quarterly* 50. 1966.

Showman, Richard K., et al., eds. *The Papers of General Nathanael Greene*. 13 vols. (Chapel Hill: University of North Carolina Press, 1976-2005.

Smith, Paul H., et al., eds. *Letters of Delegates to Congress, 1774-1789*. 26 vols. Washington, DC, 1976-2000.

Syrett, Harold C., et al., eds. *The Papers of Alexander Hamilton*. 27 vols. New York: Columbia University Press, 1961-87.

Thacher, James. *Military Journal of the American Revolution*. Hartford, CT: Hurlbut, Williams, & Company, 1862.

Willcox, William B., ed. *The American Rebellion: Sir Henry Clinton's Narrative of His Campaigns, 1775-1782, with an Appendix of Original Documents*. New Haven: Yale University Press, 1954.

SECONDARY SOURCES

Calloway, Colin G. *The American Revolution in Indian Country: Crisis and Diversity in Native America.* Cambridge: Cambridge University Press, 1995.

Chernow, Ron. *Washington: A Life.* New York: Penguin Press, 2010.

Dull, Jonathan R. *The French Navy and American Independence: A Study of Arms and Diplomacy, 1774-1787.* Princeton: Princeton University Press, 1975.

Ferguson, E. James. *The Power of the Purse.* Chapel Hill: University of North Carolina Press, 1961.

Ferling, John. *Almost a Miracle: The American Victory in the War of Independence.* New York: Oxford University Press, 2007.

_____. *The Ascent of George Washington: The Hidden Political Genius of an American Icon.* New York: Bloomsbury Press, 2009.

_____. *The First of Men: A Life of George Washington.* Knoxville: University of Tennessee Press, 1988.

Fleming, Thomas. *Washington's Secret War: The Hidden History of Valley Forge.* Washington, DC: Smithsonian Books, 2005.

Freeman, Douglas Southall. *George Washington: A Biography.* 6 vols. New York: Charles Scribner's Sons, 1949-1954.

Hughes, Rupert. *George Washington: The Savior of the States 1777-1781.* New York: William Morrow, 1930.

Knox, Dudley W. *The Naval Genius of George Washington.* Boston: Houghton Mifflin, 1932.

Lender, Mark Edward. "The Politics of Battle: Washington, the Army, and the Monmouth Campaign" in Edward G. Lengel, ed., *A Companion to George Washington.* Malden, MA: Wiley-Blackwell, 2012.

_____ and Gary Wheeler Stone. *Fatal Sunday: George Washington, the Monmouth Campaign, and the Politics of Battle.* Norman: University of Oklahoma Press, 2016.

Mackesy, Piers. *The War for America 1775-1783.* 1964. Reprint, Lincoln, NE, 1993.

Mahan, Alfred Thayer. *The Major Operations of the Navies in the War of American Independence.* 1913. Reprint, New York: Greenwood Press, 1969.

McBurney, Christian M. *The Rhode Island Campaign: The First French and American Operation in the Revolutionary War.* Yardley, PA: Westholme Publishing, 2011.

Palmer, Dave Richard. *The Way of the Fox: American Strategy in the War for America 1775-1783.* Westport, CT: Greenwood Press, 1975.

Quincy, Josiah. *The Life and Journals of Major Samuel Shaw.* Boston: Crosby and Nichols, 1847.

Rose, Alexander. *Washington's Spies: The Story of America's First Spy Ring.* New York: Bantam Books, 2006.

Ward, Christopher L. *The Delaware Continentals 1776-1783.* Wilmington: The Historical Society of Delaware, 1941.

_____ . *The War of the Revolution.* 2 vols. New York: Macmillan, 1952.

Willcox, William B. *Portrait of a General: Sir Henry Clinton in the War of Independence.* New York: Alfred A. Knopf, 1964.

Williams, Glenn F. *Year of the Hangman: George Washington's Campaign Against the Iroquois.* Yardley, PA: Westholme Publishing, 2005.

ACKNOWLEDGMENTS

N O WRITER OF HISTORY EVER TRULY WORKS ALONE. I WOULD like to thank my fellow editors, both past and present, at the Papers of George Washington and Washington Papers project at the University of Virginia. Their excellent and highly reliable work in transcribing and annotating George Washington's correspondence makes researching and writing about Washington's war in 1779 far easier that it ever could be without their volumes.

I would also like to thank Theodore Crackel, editor in chief emeritus at the Papers of George Washington, who believed in me and gave me my start as an editor of Washington's papers. Thanks also to Todd Andrlik, creator of the *Journal of the American Revolution*, and Bruce Franklin at Westholme, for giving me the opportunity to do this book. Additionally, I would like to thank Don Hagist, editor of the *Journal of the American Revolution*, for his thorough edit of the book and his great suggestions to improve the manuscript. Without you all, I could not have done this book.

I would especially like to thank my wife, Adrina, also an editor at the Papers of George Washington, for her encouragement and support while I wrote this study.

INDEX

Alexander, William (Lord Stirling), 92, 105-107, 112, 114-115, 121, 125, 127, 132-134, 136, 166n34, 170n81
Amherst, Lord, 84
Aquidneck Island, 8, 12
Arbuthnot, Marriot, 119-121, 129, 147
Archer, Henry Walgrave, 100
Armstrong, John, 110, 112

Ball, Burgess, 107, 112-113
Barbé-Marbois, Marquis de, 115-117
Bay of New York, 2
British Guards, 85
Brodhead, Daniel, 82, 159n21
Brooklyn Heights, 136
Bull's Ferry, 106-107
Butler, Richard, 98, 100

Canada, 16-18, 89
Capes of Delaware, 142
Catlett, Thomas, 113
Champion, Henry, 24
Chesapeake Bay, 83-86
Chouin, André-Michel-Victor de, 4-5
Clark, Jonathan, 107-108, 110, 112-113

Clinton, George, 16, 28, 140, 142, 167n44, 173n122
Clinton, Henry, 163n113, 164n125-126, 169n70
    attack on the Hudson and, 90
    battle of Monmouth and, 1
    decisive importance of New York and, 144
    evacuating outlying garrisons at King's Ferry and, 147
    new British strategy and, 83-94
    plans to seize the Hudson Highlands and, 119-124
    potential weaknesses of his position and, 16
    surprise at the attack on Stony Point and, 102
    Sutherland's misconduct as commandant and, 115
    troops poor health and, 137-139
    troops were sick with a "malignant jail fever" and, 120
    Washington's moves against King's Ferry and, 132
    Wayne's exploit at Stony Point and, 115
Collier, George, 85-87, 124
Connecticut militia, 93-94, 141-142
Continental Congress, 157n13, 163-164n119

Canada invasion plans and, 17
d'Estaing's intention to return to
    the North American coast
    and, 74
difficulties in clothing the army
    and, 34-35
financing the war and, 17-21
report of d'Estaing's arrival on the
    Georgia coast and, 127
situation in the Western Depart-
    ment and, 22
situation in the Western Depart-
    ment and, 22-23
trust in Washington and, 75
Washington on state of the army
    and, 63-64
Washington's desire to increase
    the strength of the army's
    regiments and, 36-37
Washington's plan of action for
    the army and, 65-68
Cornwallis, Charles, 132
Corps of Engineers, 116
Croton River, 102, 125, 132, 140
Culper spy ring, xi-xii, 13-14, 137-
    138

Delaware Indians, 80-82
Denmark, 59
d'Estaing, Charles-Hector Théodat,
    ix, 2-9, 12-14, 58, 69, 72,
    74-75, 116, 118, 124-132,
    134-135, 137-138, 142,
    145-146, 148, 167n42,
    167n44, 168n55, 169n63,
    170n77, 170n81
Dobb's Ferry, 102
Duane, James, 1, 18, 20, 76
Duportail, General, 116, 133-134,
    146, 167n45, 168n55,
    171n93, 171n102

Earl of Carlisle, 15
East River, 15, 131, 135-136
Eden, William, 15
Eightieth British Infantry Regiment,
    119

Eighty-second British Infantry Regi-
    ment, 119
English Creek, 113

Fairfax, Bryan, 57
Febiger, Christian, 98, 100
Fifth Maryland, 107
Finger Lakes, 80
First Virginia Regiment, 107, 110
Fleury, Francois Louis de, 98, 100
Flint, Royal, 24-25
Forsyth, Robert, 110, 112, 163n119
Fort Arnold, 92
Fort Lee, 106-107, 113
Fort Montgomery, 92
Fort Niagara, 18
Fort Pitt, 20, 23, 80, 82
Fort Putnam, 92
Fort Schuyler, 28
Fort Washington, 132, 135, 139
Forty-second Infantry Regiment, 85
Fourth Battalion, 104

Gates, Horatio, xiii, 2, 6, 53, 123-
    124, 135, 144, 159n14,
    167n42, 167n44, 170-
    171n89
Genesee River, 80
Gérard, Conrad-Alexandre, 69-75,
    117, 126, 142-143
Germain, George, 83-84, 119, 132
Glover, John, 94
Gordon, Cosmo, 111-112
Governor's Island, 130
Greene, Nathanael, 7-10, 35, 114,
    140, 166-167n36, 167n44,
    172n114, 172n117

Hackensack River, 106-108
Hamilton, Alexander, 2, 5, 7, 114,
    146, 166-167n36, 167n45,
    168n55, 171n93, 171n102
Handy, Levin, 107, 110-113
Harlem River, 135-136, 138
Harrison, Benjamin, 21, 43-46,
    119, 143, 145
Haverstraw Bay, 102, 124

Hay, Samuel, 100
Hazen, Moses, 140
Heath, William, 9-10, 92, 94, 121, 134-135
Hell Gate, 131, 138
Henry, Patrick, 87
Hessian Fusilier Regiment Erbprinz, 110
Hessian grenadiers, 88
Hessian Prince Charles Regiment, 85
Hessians, 85, 88, 93, 110-111, 114, 163n106, 163n113
Holker, Jean, 58
Holland, 59
Howe, Robert, 92, 101-102, 120-121, 123, 125, 132, 134, 140
Howe, William, 139
Hudson Highlands, xii, 15, 18, 92, 119
Hudson River, xii, 3, 14-15, 57, 60, 77, 87, 94-95, 104, 113, 120-121, 124, 131-132
Hull, William, 98
Hunt, Thomas, 131

Ireland, 4, 60-61, 85
Ireland Regiment, 85
Iroquois, x-xii, 19, 72, 76-77, 80, 117, 123

Jamaica Bay, 136
Jay, John, 45, 53-54, 58, 75, 82, 87, 144, 166n33
Jefferson, Thomas, 45, 50
Johnson, Henry, 95

Kalb, Johann, 92, 162n86
King's American Regiment, 93
King's Bridge, 16, 135-136, 171n94
King's Ferry, 15, 85, 87-90, 92, 94-96, 102-104, 119, 123-126, 131-134, 147, 149, 162n86, 166n34, 169-170n74, 170n77
Knox, Henry, 114, 126-127, 133

La Luzerne, Chevalier de, 115-118
Lafayette, Marie-Joseph-Paul-Yves-Roch-Gilbert de, 7-10, 12, 61, 117, 142, 145, 166-167n36, 168n51
Laurens, John, 2-3, 5
Lee, Charles, 1
Lee, Henry, 70, 100, 105-108, 110-114, 137, 163n119, 164n120
Lincoln, Benjamin, 60, 147-148
Livingston, William, 26
Long Island Sound, 6, 124, 130, 135, 137
Lord Stirling, 92, 105-107, 112, 114-115, 121, 125, 127, 132-134, 136, 166n34, 170n81
Loyalist Volunteers, 85

Mackesy, Piers, 15, 83
Malcom, William, 89
Martinique, 71
Mason, George, 45, 48
Mathew, Edward, 85-88
McDougall, Alexander, 87-88, 92, 95, 101
McIntosh, Lachlan, 22, 80
Meade, Richard Kidder, 105, 126
Miegs, Jonathan, 98
Miralles, Juan de, 69-70
Monmouth, x-xi, 1-2, 75, 153, 155n1, 166n36, 169n63
Morrisania, 135-136, 139
Mount Vernon, 49, 56
Muhlenberg, Peter, 98
Murfree, Hardy, 98

New Jersey Volunteers, 104
Newtown, battle of, 80
New Windsor, 92
New York Bay, 7, 15
New York Harbor, 124, 129, 131, 134, 138, 171n102
Nixon, John, 36, 123, 162n86
North Carolina brigade, 140

North River, 3, 85, 89, 93, 124, 171n92
Nova Scotia, 16, 129

Ottoman Empire, 59

Parliament, 40, 43, 47, 52
Parsons, Samuel Holden, 87, 93-94, 162n86
Partisan Corps, 92, 100, 107, 110, 137, 168n48
Pattison, James, 88, 110-111, 113-114, 161n68, 162n90, 163n106, 163n117, 163-164n119-120, 164n125-126
Paulus Hook, ix-xii, 15, 104-108, 112-113, 153, 163n106
Pendleton, Edmund, 45, 62, 130, 168n51
Portsmouth, 86, 119
Portugal, 59
Putnam, Israel, 87, 92, 103, 120
Putnam, Rufus, 133, 135

Randolph, Edmund, 57
Reed, Joseph, 27, 42, 143
Reid, Philip, 112-113
Robertson, James, 15, 84
Royal Garrison Battalion, 104-105
Royal Navy, 85
Rudulph, Michael, 108, 110, 113
Russia, 59

Sandy Hook, 2, 6-7, 72, 85, 130, 132, 137, 168n48, 169n63
Schuyler, Philip, 1, 77
Scott, Charles, 13, 86
Second Canadian Regiment, 140
Second Virginia Regiment, 113
Seventeenth Regiment of Foot, 88, 95
Seventy-first Regiment, 95
Seventy-sixth Regiment, 119
Shaw, Samuel, 114
Six Nations, 121, 150
Sixty-fourth Regiment of Foot, 88
Sixty-third Regiment of Foot, 88

Spain, 48, 52, 57-61, 69
Squadron of His most Christian Majesty, 14, 71
St. Clair, Arthur, 92, 127, 133, 135-136, 162n86, 166n34, 170n77, 171n92
Stewart, John, 98, 100
Stony Point, ix-xii, 88, 94-96, 98, 101-103, 105, 107, 115, 117, 123, 125, 132-135, 147, 153, 162n86, 166n25, 170n77
Sullivan, John, 7-10, 12, 58, 77, 82, 90, 121, 123, 140, 144, 153, 159n16
Supreme Executive Council of Pennsylvania, 27
Susquehanna River, 80
Sutherland, William, 105, 111-113, 115, 163n113, 164n126

Tallmadge, Benjamin, 13-14, 137-138
Taylor, John, 137
Thacher, James, 69-70
Thirty-third Regiment of Foot, 88
Townsend, Robert, 137-138
Trumbull, Jonathan, 6, 172n114, 173n128
Tryon, William, 13, 93-94, 117

Valley Forge, 64
Van Buskirk, Abraham, 104, 110, 112-113
Vaughan, John, 88
Verplanck Point, 88, 94-96, 101-102, 123, 125, 133-134, 147, 162n86, 170n77
Virginia Division, 89, 106-107, 121, 125
von Schaller, Henrich Sebastian, 110, 163n106, 163n114

Wadsworth, Jeremiah, 23-24, 141, 173n121-122
Warren, James, 50

Washington, George
    battle of Monmouth and, 1-2, 75,
        153
    British conduct of the war and,
        150-152
    change in strategy and, 142-143
    decline in patriotic zeal of citizens
        and, 21, 52
    D'Estaing's letter encouraging mil-
        itary cooperation and, 4-5
    difficulties in clothing the army
        and, 32-35, 149
    diplomacy saving the fledgling
        Franco-American alliance
        and, 8
    discussions with Continental Con-
        gress and, 16-20
    divined Clinton's strategy and,
        120
    given complete control over mili-
        tary operations and, 19-20
    identifying Clinton's strategy and,
        90
    importance of successful allied co-
        operation and, 6, 10
    lack of virtue that had taken hold
        in country and, 52-57
    letter to Benjamin Harrison and,
        46-48, 145
    letter to Benjamin Lincoln and,
        60-61
    letter to Edmund Pendleton and,
        62-63
    meeting with Delaware Nation
        and, 80-82
    need to increase the strength of
        the army's regiments and,
        36-42
    on state of the army and, 63-64
    preference for reserving opera-
        tional decisions to himself
        and, 127-128
    preparations for a direct attack on
        Staten Island and, 134
    raid on the Chesapeake and, 87
    reasons for launching the attack
        on King's Ferry and, 96

    review of the army by Gérard and
        Miralles, 70
    spy network and, xi-xii, 12-14,
        44, 121, 137-139
    states rising to the crisis and, 141-
        142
    three-day meeting at West Point
        and, 115-118
    words of praise for Lee and his
        men, 114-115
Washington, John Augustine, 69,
    76, 87, 91
Washington, Lund, 56
Wayne, Anthony, 92, 95-98, 100-
    102, 105, 107, 115, 125-
    127, 132-134, 147, 166n34,
    169n70, 170n77
West Indies, 14, 16, 47, 58, 60-62,
    74, 85, 103, 116, 122-123,
    146-148
West Point, 15-16, 23, 77, 85, 87-
    93, 101, 103, 105, 115-117,
    119-121, 123, 141-142, 147,
    149, 161n54, 162n86
Whigs, 61
Wilkinson, James, 35, 141,
    172n119
Woodhull, Abraham, 13, 138

York River, 154